FULL HOUSE / NO VACANCIES

Last Night at the *Linga Longa*

BY PAUL DAVIES

Photographs   Ruth Maddison
Director   Robin Laurie
Designer   Pippa

First produced by Theatre Works, April 1989
at *Linden*, Centre for Contemporary Arts, 26 Acland Street, St. Kilda,
(for the Melbourne Comedy Festival)

Bringing the World
Back Together

A Picture Play

Volume 8 of the Picture Play series: "*Full House/No Vacancies*"
1st Edition Published by Gondwana Press
October 2019
Suffolk Park NSW 2481 Australia

First published by Currency Press (Sydney) 1989

This book is copyright. Apart from any fair dealing for the purpose of private study, research or review, as permitted under the Copyright Act, no part may be reproduced by any process without written permission. Inquiries concerning publication, performance translation or recording rights should be addressed to the author.

Any performance or public reading of *Full House/No Vacancies* requires a licence from the author. The purchase of this book in no way gives the purchaser the right to perform the play in public, whether by means of a staged production or a reading.

© The moral right of the author has been asserted.

CONTENTS

Cast of Characters   5
Setting   6
Ground Floor Plan   7

Play Script:
    Hallway   **9**
    Sheila's Room   **13**
    Rosie's Room   **57**
    Freddie's Room   **103**
    Happy Hour (Dining Room)   **143**

Critical Reception   163

Author   183

Dedication   185

4

CAST OF CHARACTERS

Left to Right:

FREDDIE (Brian Nankervis) a forty-something stand up comic
GARETH (Merfyn Owen) a de-registered Welsh doctor
MORREY (Phil Sumner) a caretaker and invalid pensioner
SHEILA (Valentina Levkowicz) a "slightly ageing" show girl
NICK (Roger Selleck) an unscrupulous property developer
ROSIE (Carolyn Howard) a reformed prostitute
LIZ (Laura Lattuada) her friend, a former nurse, six months pregnant.

SETTING

Although it could be done on the conventional stage, *FULL HOUSE/NO VACANCIES* is designed to be performed "on location" in an actual boarding house using three bedrooms and a large TV/Dining room out the back. Scenes also take place in the central hallway.

On arrival at the house the audience is separated into three separate bedrooms (SHEILA's, ROSIE's and FREDDIE's) where events then occur simultaneously. At the end of each scene, the different audience groups rotate to a new bedroom and the simultaneous events are repeated. This is all done three times so that the three audience groups witness all three bedroom scenes - albeit in different orders.

The final scene then brings all the audience groups and all the characters together for a "Happy Hour" in the TV/Dining room out the back.

In order to facilitate the movement of characters from room to room during the simultaneous scenes, the events in each bedroom are subdivided into five units of equivalent length which are bounded by sounds heard throughout the house: clock chimes, a gunshot, SHEILA calling out, a telephone ringing, LIZ's scream, and Happy Hour music.

"LINGA LONGA" GROUND FLOOR PLAN:

Welcome To The LINGA LONGA

YOUR VIEWING ORDER FOR "FULL HOUSE/NO VACANCIES" IS:

GREEN RAFFLE TICKET

1 Freddie's Room
2 Sheila's Room
3 Rosie's Room
4 TV/Dining Room

YELLOW RAFFLE TICKET

1 Sheila's Room
2 Rosie's Room
3 Freddie's Room
4 TV/Dining Room

BLUE RAFFLE TICKET

1 Rosie's Room
2 Freddie's Room
3 Sheila's Room
4 TV/Dining Room

AFTER VIEWING EACH SCENE PLEASE WAIT TO BE USHERED TO THE NEXT ROOM

THERE WILL BE AN INTERVAL OF 15 MINUTES

FULL PROGRAMME DETAILS (WHICH INCLUDES A COPY OF THE SCRIPT) ARE AVAILABLE FROM FRONT OF HOUSE

TheatreWorks

TV/DINING ROOM

KITCHEN

TOILETS

FREDDIE'S ROOM

HALLWAY

SHEILA'S ROOM

BOOKING OFFICE

ROSIE'S ROOM

ENTRANCE

- ACLAND STREET -

Dennis, Cleaner and Front of House (Paul Davies)
also keeps the show running on time!

HALLWAY

The "Linga Longa" is an old St.Kilda rooming house that has obviously seen better times. A partially broken neon sign blinks on and off from the first storey.

Around 8pm people arrive at the front door to be confronted by a hand scrawled sign reading "Full House/No Vacancies" and a mat with the words "Wipe Ya Bloody Feet" inscribed into it. Near the door is another sign with a photo of a huge snarling dog and the caption: "Keep Out - Trespassers will be shot ! (This is no joke)". Other hand scrawled signs blu-tacked to the walls read things like: "Definitely NO BACKPACKERS!" and "Knock Loudly or Piss OFF!"

After people knock they are met at the door by MORREY the caretaker who is really annoyed.

>MORREY. (to the newcomers) YES!? (sighs impatient) What do you want?

They respond accordingly saying things like "they're here to see the show etc".

Reluctantly, MORREY opens the door and ushers them in.

> MORREY. Oh alright! Come in then! Dennis ?
> Dennis ?
> (calling out for the cleaner) Where the bloody
> hell is he?
> *Dennis*! Front door !

But DENNIS (doubling as stage manager) is nowhere to be seen. So MORREY directs people to see PATRICK (box office) in the little alcove halfway down the hallway.

Patrick at the box office.

> MORREY. Go and see Patrick then. Christ do I
> have to do everything! Dennis? Where are
> you? (looking around).

Then back to the incoming audience:

> MORREY. And don't try to steal anything. I'll
> be checking bags before you go. We've lost far
> too much cutlery this week…

So people come into a large, wide, hallway and get their raffle tickets from PATRICK which are colour coded to divide the audience into three groups (green, yellow, blue). PATRICK also gives them a map of the house which shows the order in which each group (green, yellow, blue) will see the play:

Amongst the CROWD coming in ROSIE arrives with NICK, who pays his five cents to buy some sheets of toilet paper and goes off to find the loo. While he's gone LIZ arrives with a small suitcase and backpack. She is clearly heavily pregnant. ROSIE spots her, greets her confidentially and cautiously sneaks her past MORREY into FREDDIE's room.

Also in the hallway at this point is FREDDIE FINALLY who is engaged in an increasingly depressing phone call to his agent on the public phone near the front door.

> FREDDIE. I can't believe I'm hearing this Deidre. (Listens) What do you mean you haven't got any more work for me? You owe me Deidre, you've made a bloody fortune out of me over the years. I *made* your shitty little agency and now, as soon as my career suffers a slight hiccup I'm out in the bloody cold! (Listens) I just can't believe I'm hearing this. It's ridiculous, I've been a headliner at the Last Laugh and the Comedy Cafe. (Listens) OK so I haven't been to Edinburgh I thought I'd be different. (Listens) You've taken me for granted. I just can't believe I'm hearing this! …

And so on and so forth until he slams the phone down.

> MORREY. (warning) If you break the phone you're paying for it, Finally.

> FREDDIE. (snaping back) The stupid thing is clapped out anyway.

MORREY. That's because you've been using Luna Park tokens in it!

At which point FREDDIE regrets having hung up on his agent, so he redials her number and the whole frustrated angst ridden conversation starts all over again.

We notice that FREDDIE has an arm in a sling and a black eye - two concrete examples of his latest audience reaction. These altercations between FREDDIE and MORREY continue until everyone has arrived and been assigned to a room.

At about 8.27pm the Hallway clock chimes 8.15 and events in each of the three rooms then begin happening simultaneously…

SHEILA'S ROOM

MORREY has urged people to tip-toe into SHEILA's room and remain quiet as she catches up on her regular "afternoon" beauty sleep.

Soothing, low volume music plays on her tape recorder – contrasting with the up tempo music coming from FREDDIE's ghetto blaster out in the Hallway.

While waiting we might notice, through the dim light, that SHEILA's room is jampacked with the memorabilia of years in show business: old costumes, photos of her with recognisable "personalities", theatrical posters, the odd prop or two kept for nostalgic purposes and of course a dressing table groaning with bits and pieces of makeup.

SHEILA herself lies on a large 4-poster bed.

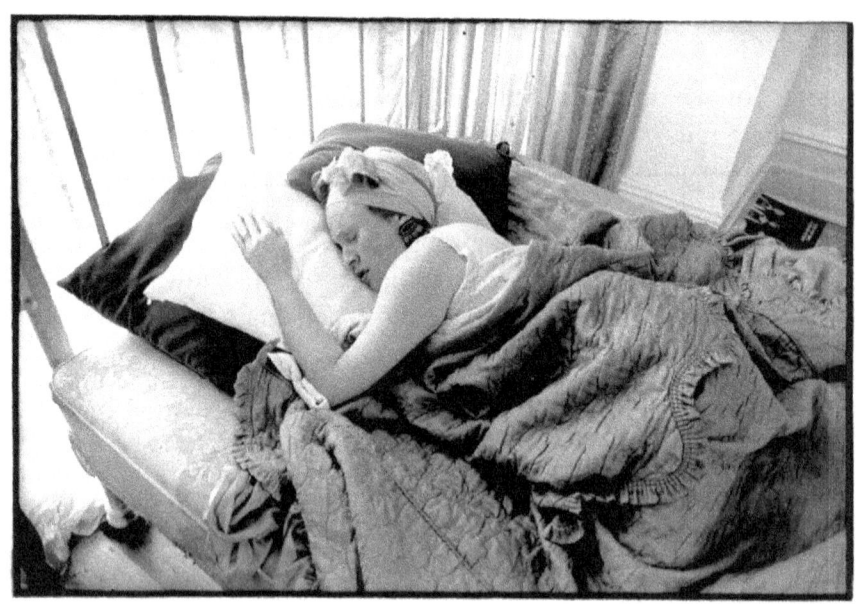

A CLOCK CHIMES 8.15 pm out in the Hallway.

Straight away an external window opens and FREDDIE's voice can be heard outside.

>   FREDDIE. (off) In here, mate. This one's
>   open.

FREDDIE climbs in through the window followed by GARETH ELWYN JONES, a stocky Welshman carrying a large white suitcase. They're LAUGHING as they soon get stuck in the narrow gap available...

FREDDIE puts his finger to his lips urging GARETH to be quiet.

>   FREDDIE. Shhhh....

They tip-toe round SHEILA's bed and FREDDIE risks a peek through the door out into the Hallway.

>   GARETH. You sure this is alright?
>
>   FREDDIE. Oh yeah.
>
>   GARETH. Why couldn't we come through the
>   front door?
>
>   FREDDIE. The bloke who runs this place is so
>   stingy he'd charge us for the air we breathe if
>   he could work out a cheap way of measuring it.
>
>   GARETH. He wouldn't really shoot
>   trespassers, would he ?
>
>   FREDDIE. Nah. (thinks about it) No I don't
>   think so.

This response hardly reassures GARETH. He doesn't look terribly comfortable.

FREDDIE risks another look round the door, and satisfied that MORREY has gone, waves GARETH forward. Together they creep out into the Hallway.

A few moments later a GUNSHOT RINGS OUT.

Shocked, SHEILA shoots bolt upright - just as MORREY hurries in carrying several plastic bags full of food.

>MORREY. Did you hear that ?

>SHEILA. What *was* that ?

He can't believe it.

>MORREY. It was a gunshot !

>SHEILA. Don't be silly, Morrey. Acland Street's all one way now. With traffic humps and licensed bistros. There may still be an unsavoury element, but you don't hear gunshots round here
>anymore.

>MORREY. Watch my lips - I - heard - a - gun – go - off !

>SHEILA. It could've been a car backfiring.

MORREY. Car be buggered it *came* from across the hallway !

SHEILA. Alright it was a gun ! What are you yelling at me for !

MORREY. It was in *her* room. It was right next door.

SHEILA. Well go and do something about it. You're the caretaker.

MORREY. I'm not going in there!

SHEILA. Why not ?

He has to think about it.

MORREY. I might get shot.

SHEILA. Then stop mincing about like a dingbat and pour me a drink.

MORREY. A gun goes off in one of my rooms and I'm not supposed to worry ?

SHEILA. Get help. Ring the police.

MORREY. I can't ring them, she's got a man in there. The cops'll think I'm running a brothel.

SHEILA. Rosie is not on the streets anymore, Morrey, She's changed her ways.

MORREY. Yes, I know, she's started bringing them home ! To *my* boarding house.

SHEILA. Are you *on* something, Morrey, or have you just
forgotten to take your medication again ?

MORREY. She's got a man in there I tell you.

SHEILA. Well, she's a grown woman and it's a free country.

MORREY. She's a dirty little scrubber and I'm a bloody fool for letting her stay here.

SHEILA. You're a fool, I won't quibble with that much.

MORREY. She knows the rules. I've told her time and again. If you've got male visitors you're supposed to leave the door open.

SHEILA. What ? So you can perve on them ?

MORREY. Don't be revolting.

SHEILA. I didn't see you leave the door open coming into my room just now.

MORREY. I can't leave the door open he might see me.

SHEILA. Morrey, you're so anxious all the time you drive me to drink.

MORREY. That'd be the day.

SHEILA. Oh forgodsake, go and get Freddie to hold your hand if
if you're too nervous about it. Call Freddie and go and knock on her door.

MORREY. Call Freddie ! That shirtlifter ! I'd rather ask a wino to mind me bottle of Grange Hermitage.

SHEILA. Freddie is a very promising young talent, you underestimate
him.

MORREY. Oh yes, he's promising alright. He's been promising me the rent since Methuselah was a boy. I mean what's with all the black? Why does he have to wear black clothes all the time? It's depressing, just looking at him.

SHEILA. He has to dress like that. It's the fashion.

MORREY. Fashion ! Pathetic. It's all veneers and surfaces. Whatever happened to that generation? Why have they lost sight of the real issues?

SHEILA. The issues have changed, Morrey.

MORREY. Fascists wear black, that's all I know.

SHEILA. He's a stand-up comic. His fans expect it.

MORREY. And about as funny as three days in bed with the dreaded lurgi.

SHEILA. If you're going to stand there whinging all night I really wish you'd do it in someone else's room - you're interrupting my warmup.

Propped up in bed, she takes her violin and starts playing it. MORREY tugs at something under her sheets.

MORREY. Speaking of which - lend us your 'lecky blanky will you Sheila ?

SHEILA. What are you doing ?

In one deft pull he rips the electric blanket out from under her and drops it on the floor. She can hardly believe it.

SHEILA. Excusé moi !

MORREY. The oven's broken down again and I've got to warm up these party pies for the Happy Hour.

SHEILA. How *dare* you !

He sniffs it, grimaces.

MORREY Augh !

SHEILA. This is disgusting.

MORREY. You're telling me! How long since you've changed the sheets ?

She jumps out of bed.

    SHEILA. Give me my blanket back.

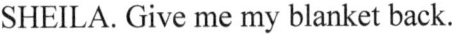

    MORREY. Are you kidding ? Have you seen the crowd that's turned up tonight ? I should make at least 30/40 cents a pie.

As he folds the electric blanket round the bags of pies she turns to her make-up table - preparing the instrument, her face.

SHEILA. Don't expect them to go off like hot cakes with my body odour soaked through them.

MORREY. You really must try and go to the laundromat more often, Sheila, instead of sitting up all day at that altar of yours like some high priestess in the church of lost causes.

SHEILA. Do I criticise your personal habits? At least I'm not afraid to go out. You're the one who's stuck in here all day. Like a bad smell.

MORREY. I am not.

SHEILA. You are, you're becoming like a little old man – a prisoner in your own home. It's that stuff you smoke. It makes you anti-social.

MORREY. You're the one who's afraid to go out!

SHEILA. I've seen your crop in the basement. It's illegal!

MORREY. I've been down Acland Street twice already today.

SHEILA. Stop avoiding the issue. You're stoned all day and night, Morrey. It affects your *brain*. Okay? You lose the will to do anything. That's why it's called *"dope"*.

MORREY. Why don't *you* take a stroll along the beach sometime, it's lovely at sunset.

SHEILA. What, and stub my toe on some junkie's needle?

MORREY slumps into an arm chair with a sigh. Almost giving up.

> MORREY You've got to open yourself up to these wider spaces occasionally, Sheila. It nourishes the soul to see that big golden orb dropping down behind the Newport Power Station - feeling the earth turn slowly beneath you. Sometimes I look at that giant chimney and it's like - like a big finger pointing straight up to God.

> SHEILA. Well I'd hate to have his lungs if he's hovering over the western suburbs.
>
> MORREY. I don't think you've been outside the building after dark as long as I've known you.
>
> SHEILA. Do you blame me with what goes on in the streets out there? You've seen those

packs of young males marauding up and down after the discos close. It's like a combat zone some nights. There's hardly a window in the whole street that hasn't been smashed by a stubbie. You know yourself you can't keep a sign up out the front before someone vandalizes it.

MORREY. If people don't goad you into it, Sheila, the only way you'll leave this room is in a box !

SHEILA. You're driving me to drink, Morrey, that's what you're doing. If my liver packs it in it's all your fault.

MORREY. If your liver packs it in it should be awarded a medal for service above and beyond the call of duty !

SHEILA. I never drink before the mid-day soap operas.

MORREY. I saw you at it just after breakfast. How anyone can wash down a nice curried mince on toast with three gin and tonics is beyond me.

SHEILA. Is that what you call it ? Mince on toast ? *Pigswill* ! Your cooking's gone right off.

MORREY. Well, nothing bloody works in there, does it ? The kitchen's turning into a disaster area.

SHEILA. Then *goad* the landlord into doing something about it! - That's what you're there for. You're the *caretaker*.

MORREY. He won't spend anymore money on the place, it's like trying to get discount from Telecom.

She helps herself to a hefty glass of punch from a large bowl.

MORREY. (disapproving) *Sheila* !

SHEILA. (innocently) I'm just testing it, Morrey, last time we had a party there was far too much ginger ale.

MORREY picks up an empty bottle of Tequila.

MORREY. Do you know how much this stuff costs ?

SHEILA. It's only Tequila.

MORREY. Enough tequila mockingbird.

They both LAUGH.

SHEILA. It's just to settle my nerves, I haven't performed in public for a long time.

MORREY. It's only a Happy Hour !

SHEILA. Only a Happy Hour!? It's a potential comeback. This could be the start of a whole new career.

MORREY. And a pretty short one if you keep sloshing it down. You'll screw your memory up. You'll end up like Rex Harrison with a radio prompt embedded in your ear, trying to sort out Hamlet from the taxi chatter: "To be or not to be…That is the cab to Hawthorn"

He laughs. SHEILA is not amused.

SHEILA. There's nothing wrong with my memory. I remember, for example that I lent you my Perry Como record to dub onto tape and that was 3 weeks ago.

MORREY. What Perry Como record ?

SHEILA. I distinctly remember handing it over to you with last
month's rent.

MORREY. This is exactly what I'm talking about - you've scorched too many brain cells.

SHEILA. Don't tell me you've lost it.

MORREY. It's embarrassing thinking of someone like you going on in
public.

SHEILA. I'm afraid you're a minority of one there, darling.

MORREY. Eh?

SHEILA. I've only just this morning auditioned for a *very* significant
cameo in a major new mini series. Any moment now I'm expecting a call from my agent.

MORREY. Hoh ! Who'd handle you ? !

SHEILA. Melbourne Talent Unlimited.

MORREY. MTU! Deidre Bleakly? Her books are closed.

SHEILA. She hinted there might even be a small cameo in one of the country's most successful teledramas.

MORREY. What Sonja Bobovich moves into Ramsay Street? I don't think so, sweetheart. *Neighbours* is a strictly a white anglo affair.

SHEILA. (coy smile) Not everyone is blind to talent, Morrey. At least some are able to detect the spirit of the girl inside the body of a mature woman.

MORREY. Mature ? - Pickled ! More like…

SHEILA. That's just water off a swan's back now, thank god. The best part about this new job is not having to put up with your smirking sarcasm any more. Oh yes, once my new mini series hits the screens I'm sure to get heaps of ads. And then I'm out of "*Linda Longa*" like a shot. I've lingered alright. I've lingered far too long in this dump.

> MORREY. You're in a prime mood tonight, what have you been lying on there, a bed of nails ?

> SHEILA. You'll pester everybody in the place except the stingy mongrel who owns it. So, as far as I'm concerned, I'm off and you can rot in hell in your broken down kitchen !

> MORREY. Alright, well, piss off then. I can't wait to disinfect this
> room and get rid of the stink.

And he storms out, SLAMMING The door hard.

SHEILA just stares at her mirror. (Wondering what all the fuss is about.) But she feels suddenly tired. But she bites her lip and goes back to putting her make-up on.

After some moments the door inches back open and a sheepish looking MORREY pokes his head around it.

> MORREY. You know I didn't mean that. (closing the door behind him) I've got a temper like a mangey dog.

She continues to ignore him.

> MORREY. It's just that - I'm used to you being here.

> SHEILA. You're *what* ?

> MORREY. Yes, alright, godamnit, I'd … I'd miss you.

> SHEILA. Am I hearing things ? Morrey Price, invalid pensioner, bares his soul ?

> MORREY. I've always cared about you, Sheila. I'd like to think we. . . well, we had a …

SHEILA. Had a what ?

MORREY. Had an understanding.

SHEILA. *MIS*understanding !

He comes forward, hesitates, then rests his hands gently on her shoulders. She stiffens, but continues to stare fixedly at the mirror.

MORREY. You've still got a pretty good bloody figure for a woman your ... age.

SHEILA (shrugging him off) What age is that ?

MORREY. Seriously, Sheila, from a certain light you, you... look like a million dollars.

SHEILA. Yeah, all green and wrinkly.

MORREY. Did I say that ? Did I ? Now who's being sarcastic ?

SHEILA. You see what you've done ? It's rubbed off on me too. Sarcasm's become an occupational hazard around here.

MORREY. Where's the passion gone ? Where's the thrill we used to share. What's happened to us Sheila ?

SHEILA. I beg your pardon ! I'm a married woman.

MORREY. We've all got our cross to bear. Just take my life - please ! A pile of yesterdays dropped like so many old newspapers in the milk crate beside the loo. Is that what it amounts to, Sheila ?

SHEILA. Oh, buck up sausage, we're going to a party, remember.

She pours herself another tumbler-full from the punch bowl. MORREY turns stern again.

MORREY. SHEILA !

SHEILA. It calms my nerves, Morrey.

MORREY. You're nervous ? (plonks a bag down beside her) Shell some peas. The Arabs have worry beads, I, Morrey Price, have peas.

SHEILA. What are these for ?

MORREY. The pie floaters of course. Be an Arab and shell some peas for me will you Sheila ? I've got a million things to do.

SHEILA. An Arab ! What a brilliant idea. I've been wondering what to wear- I'll go as … the Queen of Sheba.

MORREY. Oh sure, go as an Arab. Every costume party, there's always someone with a bit of toweling for a hat. I suppose all you can really do with a face like that is put a veil across it.

They both laugh.

SHEILA. You're lucky I'm in a forgiving mood.

She slips behind a changing screen. Clothes start appearing over the top of it.

MORREY. There's no need to go behind the screen for me, Sheila.
I'm practically blind remember.

SHEILA. If you're so blind how did you know I was behind the screen?

MORREY. It's my brilliant sense of hearing.

SHEILA. That's what I'm afraid of.

MORREY. Don't flatter yourself.

There's a DOOR SLAM off,

MORREY reacts, creeps towards the door, opens it slightly and risks a peek across the hallway then quietly slips out. Oblivious, SHEILA continues to dress behind the screen.

SHEILA (off). And so what, that's *your* costume is it ? Your bowls outfit? Really, Morrey, you could make a bit of an effort. Rosie and Freddie have gone to a lot of trouble to engender the communal spirit with this Happy Hour idea of theirs. I mean how often do you get that old singalong around the piano situation these days ? Hardly ever. Who can even play the piano ? It's a dying art form. A lost social event. In my mother's time no girl's education was complete until she could tickle the ivories. It was an essential part of wooing your beau, singing "Danny Boy" together - or "When Irish Eyes Are Smiling". Now all they've got is these damn Sony walkman things - completely cut off from all human contact You're always critical of her, but if it wasn't for Rosie, life round here would be very dull indeed. And I'm serious about leaving you know. I only came here for a two week rest between engagements and that was 10 years ago.(reflecting back, becoming nostaligic) Funny how you become stuck in a place without realising it. You settle in, get comfortable, establish a proper relationship with the Lebanese family at the local milk bar and suddenly it's ten Christmases later. Morrey ?(slight pause) *Morrey* ?

She emerges as the Queen of Sheba. Her costume complete, looking around for him and an admiring response.

SHEILA. (realises he's gone, disappointed) *Morrey* !

She storms over to the door, opens it and yells into the hallway.

SHEILA. *Where's my perry como record* !!!

She exits, slamming the door behind her.

Immediately she's gone the window opens and NICK CARTWRIGHT staggers through, falling onto the floor. All he's got on is a short, silky dressing gown. His hairy legs wildly inappropriate for the garment.

NICK picks himself up nervously from the floor, spots the wardrobe and rummages into it, throwing out all SHEILA'S weird and wonderful costumes, looking for something vaguely decent to put on.

He pauses over a Perry Como record for a moment before throwing it away.

Clothes-wise though, all he can find is women's stuff.

Despairingly, he holds up a dress just as a great, hairy black gorilla bursts in through the door, carrying a large white suitcase.

>NICK. Holy Shit !

The gorilla also reels back in fright.

>GORILLA. Huh?

NICK holds the dress defensively in front of him.

>GORILLA. (with GARETH's unmistakable Welsh accent) Sorry, mate. . . (takes in the room) er … madam…

>NICK. (affronted) What ?

The gorilla peels his head off - revealing GARETH who we saw come through the window with FREDDIE earlier.

>GARETH. Didn't mean to disturb you.

NICK is mortified at being sprung like this. He quickly flings the dress away.

>NICK. *Madam* !

>GARETH. Wrong room, lady, sorry.

GARETH moves to make an equally brief exit through the window.

34

Furious, NICK grabs GARETH by the chest fur, threatening him.

NICK. I'm a bloke you bastard !

GARETH. Yeah. And I'm a gorilla.

GARETH LAUGHS.

NICK. Are you *listening to me* !

NICK is not amused.

GARETH. Alright, you're a bloke, I'm a bloke,
we're all blokes
together.

NICK releases his grip instantly, even more appalled.

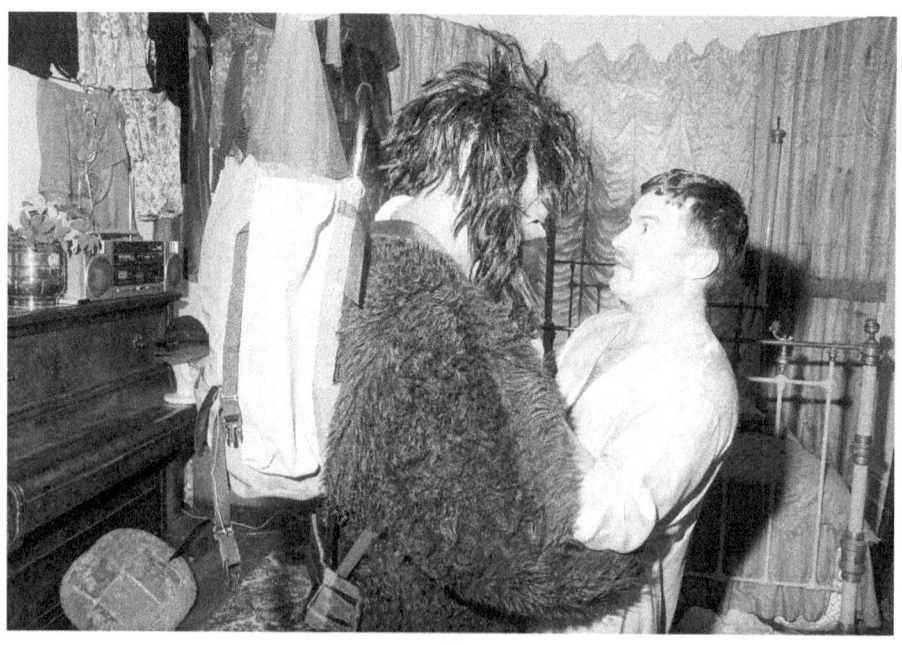

NICK. Hang on - I'm not ... (gay)!

GARETH. Look, mate, whatever you are is fine by me. I just want you to know that I respect your right to dress as a woman.

NICK. SHUT UP!

GARETH. I think society should too.

NICK. (breaking down) I only came here for a cup of coffee.

GARETH. Sorry, can't just now - in a bit of a rush. Thanks, anyway.

NICK. I'm really normal.

GARETH. Of course you are.

NICK. She took my clothes!

GARETH. Hang on.

GARETH feels something deep inside the gorilla costume. He reaches one hand in through the main zip at the front and starts rummaging around…

GARETH. There's something long and sinewy down here - like a,
like a baby's arm with an apple on the end of it.

He extracts from his gorilla costume a long, thick bullwhip.

GARETH stares at it in amazement.

GARETH. Good god!

NICK. (backing off) I'm *definitely* not into *that*!

> GARETH. (regarding the whip) No, I'm more a sheep man myself.

> NICK (panicking) Jesus !

NICK gives GARETH a wide berth, circling round him, edging nervously towards the door.

> GARETH. Shearing, you know. Outback ? If I ever get there.

He steps forward to shake hands

> GARETH, Gareth Wynn-Jones.

NICK is reeling back, holding his arms up in front protectively. Hoping to fend GARETH off.

> NICK. Please don't hit me !

He slips through the door and is gone.

> GARETH. Isn't that what you call it, the great outback ? Behind the black stump. Near the tucker box, outside Gundagai. I'm just down under for the season. From Wales. . .

He looks around but NICK is gone.

> GARETH (slightly peeved) Friendly bloody lot. Thanks for your welcome, cobber. Come over to our country some time, make yourself at home. 'Least we talk to people. Shake their hand. I wouldn't want you to strain yourself.

GARETH spots the punch bowl.

> GARETH. Would you like a drink ? (offering it to himself) Thanks old sport, don't mind if I do.

GARETH recharges SHEILA's glass just as her phone starts RINGING.

He freezes. Puts the glass down. Looks anxiously around the place – if a phone's ringing somebody's probably going to come and answer it. And sure enough a moment later the door swings open.

GARETH disappears behind her screen just as SHEILA re-enters, breathless.

> SHEILA. The agency !

She looks down at her ridiculous costume checks it in the mirror and realises that it *is* ridiculous. Panicked, she races behind the screen again to throw something more respectable on, then scrambles round the dressing table for some lipstick- just as the phone stops. Obviously, but curiously she failed to notice GARETH hiding behind her screen.

SHEILA is aghast.

> SHEILA. What am I doing ? It was only a phone call. What a ludicrous woman you are. The first serious job in three years and you throw it away like some nervous virgin. Because you didn't look right.

Then a new thought.

> SHEILA. I'll ring them back. I was in the shower, I heard the phone ... but I couldn't get to it. I'll ring them back and just ask them straight out. That can't hurt. You can't be afraid of ringing people up. The streets at night is one thing, but you can't be timid about phones in this day and age. That's what they're there for. People wouldn't have them if they didn't want you to ring them back. Especially agents. That's their job isn't it? Taking calls ... putting you on hold. (depressing realisation) Fobbing you off.

She turns away from the mirror

> SHEILA. I can't ring them back. It'll make me sound desperate. They'll think I'm too keen. Not getting enough work. Obviously past it. I couldn't bear it- Morrey gloating, leering at me with that retarded, I-told-you-so look of his. How humiliating. It's out of the question. Oh why haven't I got an answer machine !

The phone rings again. She tenses, torn between relief and anxiety.

> SHEILA. Let it ring a few times. Don't want them to think I'm overly anxious.

She takes a deep breath, composes herself then snatches it quickly.

SHEILA (composed voice) Sheila Dwyer speaking.

Her expectations crumble.

SHEILA. Oh - Father Brosnan. (unenthused)
Hullo father.
(listens)
Yes, long time no see.
(listens)

SHEILA. Well, yes, I have been meaning to come to mass, father, it's just that I've been a little off colour lately.
(listens)
No, no nothing serious. Look, father, I don't suppose... you didn't try and ring me just a moment ago did you ?
(listens)
No ? It's just that I'm expecting an awfully important call, and I do imagine things are rather busy for you at this very Christian time of the year.
(listens)
Well- you know, Easter and all that. .
Don't tell me you'd forgotten.
(laughs)
Yes, well, best not to hold you up, father.

She goes to hang up but can't quite extricate herself from the conversation. Seizing an opportunity to sneak away the gorilla creeps a step or two outside the screen, but dashes back because SHEILA half turns towards it as the conversation continues.

SHEILA. What father ? A proposition ? I hope it's not rude.
(laughs)
As I always say, father "Love thy neighbour, but don't
get caught."
(laughs)
No, I'm always thrilled to hear from you, father.
(listens)
Of course, I'd love to help the boys and girls in the Holy Name Society, but what can I ...? (listens)
Oh. I see, a concert, yes
(her mood drops)
Well, yes. . .
(listens)

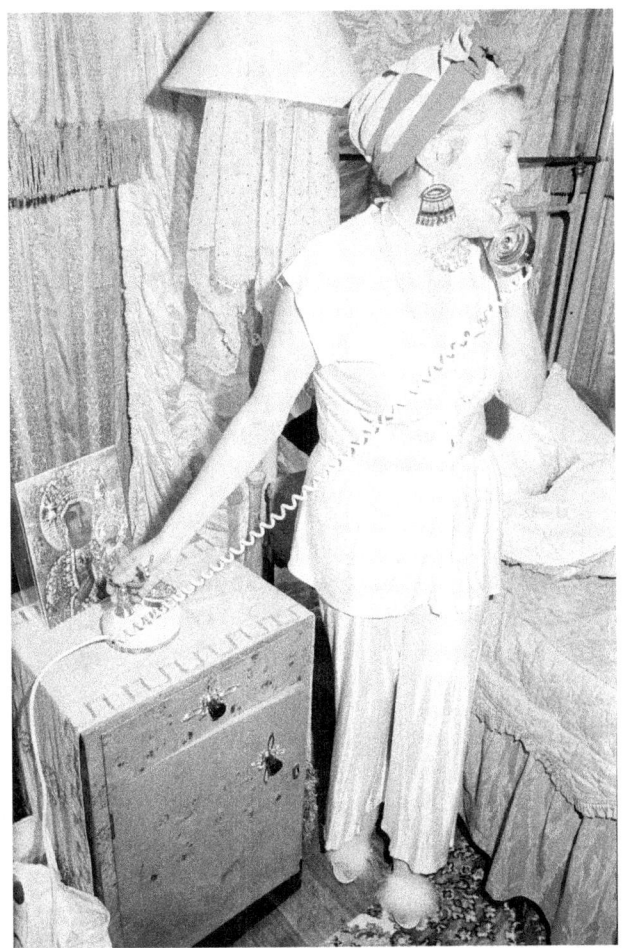

SHEILA. Yes, of course, it's a wonderful way to raise money, it's just that I haven't quite dusted off the old repertoire for so long, father I. .
(listens)
Well, yes, I believe

For the first time she notices her clothes scattered all over the floor. Then back to the phone call.

SHEILA. (listens)
Yes.
(listens)

Yes..

    (listens)
    Well, yes. . . it's just that I'm rather flat out at
    the moment father.
    (listens)
    Yes.
    Yes, father, yes.
    (listens)

While continuing to talk SHEILA stands and regards the disorder of her wardrobe more closely, frowning.

    SHEILA. Yes, of course father, yes.
    (listens)
    I agree, absolutely.
    (listens)
    Yes, well, its funny you should ask really,
    because after all these years I've just been
    invited to tour with the Adelaide Theatre
    Company.
    (listens)
    The ATC father. They've asked me to be their
    Hedda for a national tour.
    (listens)

Still talking, she follows the stream of clothes to behind the screen and without seeming to notice anything unusual goes on talking as she gathers clothes around and behind it. Trying to restore some order.

    SHEILA. Yes, I'm afraid I'll be interstate for
    some weeks.

She crosses herself seeking pre-emptive redemption for the lie.

    SHEILA. (listens)
    Yes.
    (listens)
    Yes.
    (listens)
    Yes.

> (listens)
> Yes, well, *do* call me again if I can be of any help in the future.
> (listens)
> Yes. .
> (listens)
> Yes, father, yes.
> (listens)
> Yes. .
> Yes ... goodbye.

With a huge sigh she re-emerges from behind the screen and starts hanging her clothes back in the wardrobe.

> SHEILA. Some people just won't take "NO" for an answer.

She stops, looks quizzically back at the screen, thinking about it. Shakes her head, then notices MORREY's pies still sitting on her bed. She unplugs the blanket and throws the bundle contemptuously into her lounge chair.

She turns back to the mirror.

> SHEILA. I can't possibly wear this, this looks ridiculous.

She reaches to recharge her drink only to discover to her surprise that the glass is full. She holds it out from her.

While she's looking at the glass GARETH, seizing his chance makes an exaggeratedly quiet tip-toe out the door.

Just as soon as he's gone, SHEILA thinks she notices something strange in the mirror, she swings round but there's nothing behind her.

That's odd.

She turns back to the mirror, frowns, gets up, goes tentatively behind the screen.

Suddenly we hear LIZ'S SCREAM off in another room.

SHEILA freezes behind the screen.

The door suddenly opens and FREDDIE backs in, crouching over as he peeks nervously back out into the Hallway through a narrow opening in the door.

She spots him through a crack in her screen.

> SHEILA. Freddie ! Where's my money ?
>
> FREDDIE. Sssh…(whispers) Sheila…

He softly closes the door.

> SHEILA. Don't sush me, you owe me for being your laugh starter.
>
> FREDDIE. I can't deal with that now, Sheila, I'm in the midst of
> a personal crisis.
>
> SHEILA. Come on. $20 a show. That's what you promised. It's the
> hardest work I've ever done trying to laugh at your jokes.
>
> FREDDIE. Yes, and where were you tonight ? It was awful. I *died* on stage. The audience was like Ayers Rock. Big, red, bloated and stoney faced.
>
> SHEILA. (noticing the sling) What happened to your arm ?
>
> FREDDIE. I felt like a turkey two weeks before Christmas.

SHEILA. And your coat, what's this ? Dried carrot ?

She flakes off some stuff from his lapel.

FREDDIE. Just a bit of *feed*back from one of
the tables up the front. Pun intended.

SHEILA. They threw food at you ?

FREDDIE. Well in a manner of speaking, yes,
I suppose they did.
They opened their mouth ... and out it came.

SHEILA is appalled.

SHEILA. I didn't think stand-up comedy was
supposed to be a
hazardous occupation.

FREDDIE. A night out in Niddrie would've
been funnier than that lot.

SHEILA. That's just your persecution complex.

FREDDIE. You're only saying that 'cause you
hate me.

SHEILA. Look, go and get yourself a nice safe
job in television.
You can do it, you're a natural.

FREDDIE. A natural disaster. I'm so depressed
I feel like the sludge
at the bottom of an elbow pipe.

SHEILA. You're not having a mid-life crisis
are you, darling ?

FREDDIE. What's mid-life ? For poor buggers
like me it's probably

only about 19 or 20.

He goes to open one of her many bottles of spirits. Helping himself.

>SHEILA. You're going to be in a fine mood for the Happy Hour.

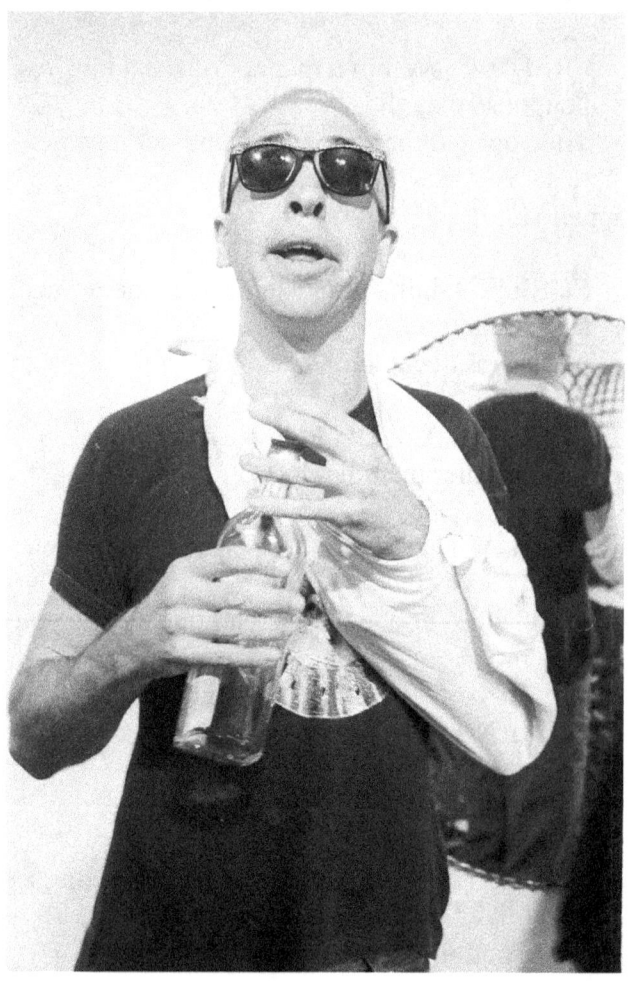

>FREDDIE. "Happy" ? - I'm sorry, is that a word I should know ?

>SHEILA. You're too bleak, Freddie. Everything about you is a downer. Get a new

costume, change your name. What sort of label is "Freddie Finally" anyway, I mean, "finally" what ?

FREDDIE. Finally ratshit.

SHEILA. (giving up) Oh !

He falls back into her bed.

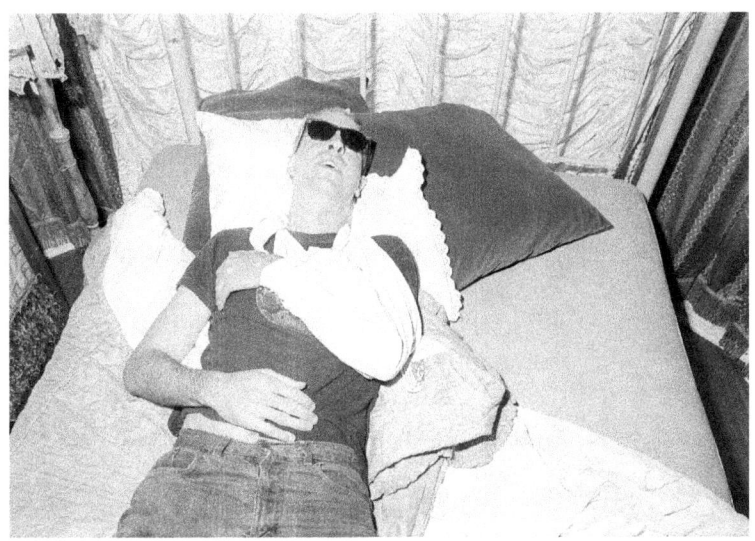

FREDDIE. Perhaps I could just go to bed for three years.

SHEILA. Why don't you try something more upbeat- like "Randy Pratt" or- "Laughlin McLaughlin" ?

FREDDIE. I knew a Laughlin McLaughlin once. That's how bad my childhood was. (looking around) Is there anything to eat ? I'm starving.

He drops himself into the chair with the party pies. SHEILA screams out in horror- but she's too late.

SHEILA. (pulling him up) Get off, get off!

She opens the blanket to reveal the squashed pies.

SHEILA. Oh look at that! How am I going to keep warm tonight?

FREDDIE. (putting an arm around her) You could always sleep with a friend.

SHEILA. Sleep with a con artist.

FREDDIE. 'Least I won't give you tinea, not like Morrey.

SHEILA. I don't know why everybody thinks Morrey and I have anything in common.

FREDDIE. You won't leave him then? For someone younger?

SHEILA. (shrugging him off) Get out of it.

FREDDIE. Actually, Sheila, I've come to ask you to star in my movie.

SHEILA. How much is this going to cost me?

FREDDIE. An Australian woman pilot, shot down in Vietnam…

SHEILA. Are you serious?

FREDDIE. Jane Fonda saw her when she went to Hanoi in 1969.

FREDDIE goes into presumptive director mode

FREDDIE. Imagine the opening scene, a crippled B52 coming into Saigon airport, Pink Floyd on the sound track …

SHEILA. (warming to the idea) Is Brian Brown going to be my co-star?

FREDDIE. Brian Brown and Jack Thompson will be *competing* for you.

She allows herself to get excited.

SHEILA. Oooh…

Then thinks about it.

SHEILA. I wouldn't want Brian to get disappointed if he misses out.

FREDDIE returns to his theme.

FREDDIE. Underneath the B52, choppers and F14s are engaged in a furious firefight. Rocket propelled grenades trace white trails of toxic phosphorous as they plunge into the jungle...

SHEILA. What sort of budget did you have in mind for this thing?

FREDDIE. All I need is $400 to buy the camera.

SHEILA. Get out of here.

FREDDIE. Alright, Sheila, I'll be perfectly frank …

SHEILA. Why break the habit of a lifetime?

FREDDIE. I've got this mate who needs a loan.

SHEILA. I don't know why you're looking at me.

FREDDIE. 'Cause he's a Celt, Sheila - like you - a poor little Welshman who's lost his passport, money, everything. He helped me tonight when I was getting bashed up.

SHEILA. I'm not made of money, you know.

FREDDIE. Sheila, he's a Red Dragon of the Free Welsh Army. He's come out here to raise support for the Welsh people's legitimate struggle against the forces of Saxon (imperialism)

SHIELA. (cutting him off) You want cash - go and do some ads.

FREDDIE. You're asking me to sell my integrity ?

SHEILA. I thought you said you didn't have a conscience.

FREDDIE. Have you actually watched television lately ? Do you realise that half of what most people now see of human behaviour is scripted ?

SHEILA. You could always do voice overs for the wax museum.

FREDDIE. I'm 40 years old! Sheila.

SHEILA. We've all got our problems, darling.

FREDDIE. Today ! 40 years old today ! (starts breaking down) My 40th birthday. And no one remembered !

SHEILA. People are busy, Freddie, you can't expect them to remember every little detail.

FREDDIE. Are you listening to me !? I'm having a titantric personal crisis here. (getting the sense of it mixed up)

SHEILA. You're only as old as the person you're feeling, sweetheart.

FREDDIE. Excuse me, I find that inference offensive…

SHEILA. Look at Sidney Poitier - still playing teenagers well into his 30s.

FREDDIE. (voice grinding down, like his spirit) I can't go on anymore, Sheila. I just can't cut it up there. I'm tired of always working some shithouse pub or bowlo where the bouncers look like Russ Hinze and your eyes are weeping and your lungs are screaming from an impenetrable smog of cheap cigarettes. The p.a.'s always on the blink and the audience is some drunken rifle club. Or a bucks night in Bilowela. I'm 40 years old Sheila. Is this all it amounts to ?

SHEILA. Alright ! You've had a rough night. Who hasn't ?
So pick yourself up off the floor, Freddie.

FREDDIE. I can't, my shoes are always stuck to the carpet.

SHEILA. Look, if your Ford Zephyr carks it, Freddie, all you've got to do is stick your thumb out - or hail a cab. If you give up at the first sign of trouble you'll be stuck on the side of the road forever.

FREDDIE. That's what I'm telling you, Sheila, *I can't do it anymore*. I just can't cut the mustard. My career, my life is over !

SHEILA. Hoh ! Life ! You know what life is ? Life is a sexually transmitted disease.

FREDDIE. And it's *terminal*.

SHEILA. Excuse me - is this the people's poet speaking ? The radical cabaret artisté? The uncensored voice of the cultural revolution ? The stand-up comic who was going to change the world ?

FREDDIE. It's no good Sheila, I've lost it. I'm Tony Hancock in that final motel room. I'm Lenny Bruce busted for the 18th time. I'm Dylan Thomas in America. (breaking down) I can't even do a Happy Hour in my own boarding house.

SHEILA. Yes, you've lost it alright. If that's your attitude. You're good for nothing but the compost heap Freddie if you've forgotten that tingle you get when an audience laughs with you, when you see their faces light up… that sense of power you get when you hold the mirror up.

FREDDIE. A mirror image is always false Sheila. It looks the same
but actually reversed.

SHEILA. What did you ever really aspire to ? The sound of your own voice ? Some stupid idea about being a star ? You're just like all the other little prima donna's in this business, darling: so enamoured of your own ego you've even lost sight of the passion, that gift, that drove you to seek the limelight in the first place

FREDDIE. No ! That's a lie.

SHEILA. Is it?

She turns his head forcing him to look in her mirror.

SHEILA. Look at you ! It's pathetic. (pushing his head forward, almost bashing him) Go on take a good look at yourself. Freddie Finally, alright. Finally a washed up whimp. One hard night and you're carrying on like some spoilt brat who's just lost his favourite toy.

FREDDIE. Not just *one*, Sheila. Heaps of nights. Weeks of it. Months of stuffing disasters. Nothing but blank stares and a deafening silence.

SHEILA. Alright, so who's counting? Not me. Who cares whether you die on stage. No one, sweetheart. Ultimately. We're all alone up there. No props, no babysitters to hold your hand. Just you and whatever talent you've managed to claw from years of near hits and direct misses and the occasional thrill of an extended season. I cared about you once because I thought you had some fire in your belly.

FREDDIE. I was only ever an artiste for my ideas.

SHEILA. I don't care what you *were* Freddie. What you *were* is irrelevant. What you *were* is a scrapbook of fading reviews.

FREDDIE. I used to think I was wishy washy - now I'm not so sure.

SHEILA. Morrey's right, you're a card carrying member of the do-nothing generation. The me, me, me, me society.

FREDDIE. Morrey's wrong. He's always wrong.

SHEILA. Then prove it ! This Happy Hour is your opportunity. Your comeback moment. Show them that you've still got it, Freddie. Take a risk, be bold. If you don't change you die.

FREDDIE. How, how can I change ?

SHEILA. I don't know … Put a funny nose on. Wear a wig. Stand back from the audience and give yourself a mask to hide behind if that's what you need. But get back in that Ford Zephyr now or you'll never drive again.

1930s/40s DANCE MUSIC can be heard drifting in from the start of the Happy Hour out in the dining room. As SHEILA opens the door it gets louder.

>   SHEILA. There's your cue, Freddie. Take it, take it now ! Seize the moment. Go out there a moderately successful pub artiste and come back a *star* !

She ushers him towards the door, he hesitates, she leads him on.

>   FREDDIE. (terrified) Oh Christ ! (following her out)

ROSIE'S ROOM

The mood in ROSIE's room is subdued, tasteful and mildly erotic - heavy with the scent of cheap perfume.

Although it is a bit hard to see when we first come in (because the room's in blackout) there's a large wardrobe and a rather spartan "bed" (like a door on four legs) which could almost be a kind of massage table. Above it several Chinese posters indicate acupuncture points, muscular systems etc.

As soon as people are settled a clock outside CHIMES 8.15 pm.

The door opens and ROSIE switches the light on as she ushers in a shy, rather nervous young man dressed in a very conservative suit, carrying some flowers, an umbrella, and an expensive looking briefcase. He gives the impression he could've come straight from work at the stock exchange.

    ROSIE. Are you sure you're feeling OK ?

NICK. Yeah, I'm fine.

ROSIE. You seem ...

NICK. What ?

ROSIE. I dunno- out of sorts.

NICK. Rubbish, I'm brilliant.

He smiles thinly, shyly hands her the flowers.

ROSIE. For me ?

NICK. I had them in the car.

ROSIE. (taking them) Thank you, they're lovely.
(sniffs them) I adore beautiful things.

NICK. Well, you are beautiful.

They share a modest smile.

NICK seems kind of lost as to what to do next.

ROSIE. Would you like the "general relaxation" or is there some specific problem ? Polo-shoulder, computer-neck ?

NICK. No "general relaxation" sounds great.

She touches him gently on the chest.

>NICK. (almost starting from her touch).
>Actually, I have got a bit of tennis elbow to be perfectly frank.
>
>ROSIE. Why don't you slip into something more comfortable
>while I put these in water and ... oil my hands.

He gulps slightly and she hurries out with the flowers.

As soon as she's gone he places his briefcase and umbrella on a small table, opens the briefcase, takes out a gun, looks at it for a moment, sighs, looks at the door aims at the door as if waiting for her to come back, then lowers his arm and slowly turns the barrel on himself.

He puts the gun in his mouth, closes his eyes, but it tastes terrible so he takes it out again. Then he holds it out in front of him - as far away as his violently shaking hands can reach. He squeezes his eyes closed, his body convulsing.
Finally he pulls the trigger.

A GUNSHOT RINGS OUT.

He opens his eyes.

> NICK. Missed !

Drops the hand holding the gun and sinks onto "the bed"

> NICK. Can't even bloody kill myself.

Suddenly he becomes aware of the noise he's caused, he looks at the gun, looks around for a place to ditch it and quickly slips it under a pile of magazines.

He sits for a moment then turns back to the magazines, there's several copies of "Playboy" "Penthouse" "Kharma Sutra" "Girls Own Annual" etc. Vaguely interested he picks one up and flicks through it.

Stirred a little by this he puts the magazine back, stands, loosens his tie and slowly strips down to his jocks and sox folding his suit over a chair with an almost anally retentive correctness, pressing every seam and making sure there are no creases. Despite the suit however he wears rather bizarre underpants. After a moment he realises this so he peels them off to reveal a more normal pair underneath.

Considers them, then pulls them off again to reveal a third, bizarre pair again.
Undressing completed he turns to the bed, tentatively he sits on it then lies back.

He vainly tries to adopt an alluring, sexy pose, trying the haughty "roman nobleman on one elbow" position, then the "come and get me palms behind his head" idea and so on - with a couple of other poses - all of which he seems unsatisfied with until he rolls sideways and comes eye level with a small condom dispensing machine. That's certainly something he hadn't thought about.

He gets up on an elbow, considers the choice, his hand moving from the "Small" chute to the "Large" chute before finally settling for the "Medium"- one of which he takes and, after wondering where he's going to put it, slips it into a sock.

He then returns to the sexy anticipatory reclining pose again, albeit a bit more confidant now. But a secondary thought prompts him to sit up again. His conscience gets the better of him and he takes a "Small" condom just to be honest, and slips this into his other sock.

He regards his two socks. Crosses his legs, small on top medium below, then decides to reverse this and waits again.

Still no sign of ROSIE.

He finishes with the posing, then fully lies back on the bed and fully relaxes for the first time ... before getting a shock from the full length mirror suspended above the "bed".

He checks his watch. Exhales a loud breath. Lies back on the bed and looking up at the mirror becomes aware for the first time of the pillow that he's lying on.

He sits up, pulls the pillow around on top of his knees, sniffs it, rubs his cheek along it, caressing it, burying his face in it. He seems entranced by its luxurious softness, exploring the texture, the delicious scent of her body on it, almost making love to it, hugging it, kissing it. ... until we hear the window rattling and

FREDDIE's voice off.

>FREDDIE. (off) Hey, mate, this one's open.

NICK freezes like a rabbit caught in the shooter's spotlight. He leaps off the bed, and faces the window, terrified, flinging the pillow away from him.

He looks down at his jocks - no time to do anything about that now. So he races to switch off the light and hides in the wardrobe...

... just as the window opens and we hear FREDDIE and GARETH clambering in, laughing at the sillyness of it all. Someone drops a couple of stubbies.

>FREDDIE. Careful of the grog, mate.

>GARETH. Sorry cobber.

LAUGHTER again.

>FREDDIE Sshhh!

FREDDIE flicks the lights back on.

As we've seen before, FREDDIE has his arm in a sling and a rather prominent black eye. The sling doubles as a convenient stubbie holder. GARETH is standing in the middle of the room carrying more stubbies and a large white suitcase. He takes in the erotic paraphernalia.

GARETH. (whistles approvingly) This is yours?

FREDDIE. Cut it out.

GARETH. Nice decor.

FREDDIE. Belongs to a friend of mine.

GARETH. Remind me to say "hullo."

FREDDIE. It's safer in here till I can sneak you into my place. The caretaker's a real bastard. He keeps charging me extra for having friends over.

GARETH. I don't want to be a hassle.

FREDDIE. Never let it be said an Aussie wouldn't help his mate, mate.

GARETH. Right, mate.

FREDDIE. Besides, you'll need a costume for the party and Rosie's got the best stuff.

FREDDIE opens the wardrobe door, quickly rummaging through leather studded gear, fishnet stockings, dog collars etc.

FREDDIE. Seriously, I owe you for tonight, man.

GARETH. (dismissive) Ah !

FREDDIE. Especially taking me to casualty - waiting there the four hours and everything.

GARETH. (shrugs) 'Least I could do.

FREDDIE. Not many blokes would leap into a pub brawl to help a someone they don't even know.

GARETH. You were out numbered. It seemed unfair.

FREDDIE. Pretty embarrassing audience response really - getting half kicked to death in front of the stage.

GARETH. Somebody thought it was part of the act.

FREDDIE. What's happening to people nowadays ? No one cares anymore. It's just this moral decline. There's no *substance*, no *guts* to anything.

>GARETH. It wasn't a bad show, mate.

>FREDDIE. I had 'em GARETH, I had 'em in the palm of my hand.
>Until that silly joke about the colostomy bottle.

>GARETH. I was laughing. .

FREDDIE looks hurt.

>GARETH. ... Er - before you ah, got beaten up.

>FREDDIE. Hope to Christ my agent never finds out. She's been looking for an excuse to chuck me off her books for ages. It's insane. I can't believe It. I *made* that ratshit agency. I was a headliner at Jokes Incorporated. Now she wants a guaranteed 500 bucks a year - from ME ! A founding member of the Comedy Supermarket ! I've even sold jokes to Mort Sahl. Ok, so I haven't been to Edinburgh. Who wants a lot of people in kilts laughing at you? But now, when my career strikes a little rough patch, it's like I'm an albatross or something. I mean, Mort Sahl for chrissake ! Where's the loyalty ? Where's the, substance ?

>GARETH. Down the gutter and out the drain.

>FREDDIE. I can cop a bashing but when that bastard started taking
>photos...

>GARETH. That was callous.

>FREDDIE. They protect paintings from flash cameras - why not artists ?

FREDDIE finally picks out a gorilla suit from ROSIE's wardrobe.

>FREDDIE. Brilliant. Try that on for size.

>GARETH. (reeling back) You're not serious.

>FREDDIE. No, mate, no. I'm a comedian.
>(laughs, swigs from his stubbie)

>GARETH. I can't wear that.

>FREDDIE. Everyone else'll have a costume on.

>GARETH. What ?

As FREDDIE turns away from the wardrobe to bundle GARETH into the Gorilla suit we see NICK's trembling hand shoot out from inside the wardrobe to close the door.

>FREDDIE. For the party. We have this little get together every 3rd Tuesday (adjust). Just a few friends round the piano, a bit of show and tell, Sheila plays keyboards, I crack a few jokes, it's become a real event.

GARETH turns back to the mirror in the wardrobe door, neither of them seem conscious of the fact that it's closed itself.

>GARETH. Don't you think I might stand out a bit in this ?

>FREDDIE. It's the perfect disguise. Hidden in plain sight.

>GARETH. But I'm allergic to nylon.

>FREDDIE Morrey'll never pick you.

FREDDIE completes the costume by putting the head on.

FREDDIE. You animal, eh ? (laughs) You'll drive the women wild.
They love an untamed beast occasionally.

FREDDIE takes another swig of beer, passes the stubbie to GARETH.

FREDDIE Great. (laughs)

FREDDIE starts fixing his own costume up in the mirror.

FREDDIE. So you're just over on a visit are you ?

GARETH. What ?

FREDDIE. From old Blighty ?

GARETH. Oh - no, no, I'm from Wales.

FREDDIE. I knew it ! I thought I detected a slight musical lilt.

GARETH. You wouldn't believe what's happened to me since nine o'clock yesterday: the jumbo's late leaving Bangkok so the curfew stops us landing in Sydney and by the time we divert to Melbourne all the baggage handlers have knocked off for the night. I've got the wrong suitcase, no passport, my wallet's been stolen, a cousin waiting to greet me in Sydney and absolutely no means of getting there.

FREDDIE. You can't wire home for something ?

GARETH. I can't identify myself to go and collect it.

FREDDIE. Welcome to Australia, mate. A land of bloody thieves.

GARETH. Yeah. Well -

FREDDIE. There's no need to be coy about it.
That's a bloody fact.
I'll bet you lost your wallet at my gig, right?

GARETH. I think so. In the toilet.

FREDDIE. Pack of convicts. I should've burnt
the place down.

GARETH. Like the Free Welsh Army.

FREDDIE. Who?

GARETH. Bunch of smart boyos from home.
They torch English holiday houses in Wales -
but only when no one's there. So no one's ever
hurt and the bloody bobbies can't for the life of
them twig to who's doing it.

FREDDIE. Brilliant !

GARETH. I'll tell you what, it keeps the price of an old Welsh cottage nice and accessible for ordinary people - 'least them as haven't got much to start with.

FREDDIE. (reaching for his wallet) Listen, I'd like to help you out, mate.

GARETH. No, no, no.

FREDDIE. No, I insist. How much do you need ?

GARETH. Well, I can't get my passport replaced till I find 100 dollars, and of course I can't get that till I have a passport, which means a lot of expensive telephone calls. Say - 150.

FREDDIE. (gulps, closes his wallet) Oh well, if you insist. But don't worry about tonight, right. There's a bed in my room - it's yours. Tomorrow we can put the hard word on Sheila or Rosie, they're loaded.

GARETH. I can't impose myself on you like this.
FREDDIE. Look, I owe *you* mate, consider it fixed.

GARETH. No, no, I'll just walk around for a few hours, might get a kip on the beach tomorrow.

FREDDIE. Not in that gorilla suit you won't. (laughs, pressing his keys upon GARETH)

GARETH. That's awfully kind of you but …

FREDDIE. *Take* my room ! I'm sure to score tonight. I won't need it.

This reminds FREDDIE, he helps himself to a couple of small condoms from ROSIE's dispenser.

FREDDIE. I mean, I'm doing a gig aren't I ?
There's always someone
in the audience wants to take me home.
(remembering his manners)
Er - some for you ?

GARETH. What ?

FREDDIE. Small ? Medium ?

GARETH. Oh - no I don't think so.

FREDDIE. Better to be safe than sorry.

GARETH. Do you think we should just take them ?

FREDDIE. Oh, Rosie doesn't mind, she's happy to give them away. My god ! We've all got a *duty* to give them away. (holding one up) Powerful medicine, mate. These little things actually brought down a fascist regime in Queensland.

GARETH. Oh, well - ahm, one night - half a dozen large I think.

FREDDIE. Hoh !

FREDDIE chucks them over.

FREDDIE. Welshmen, eh ? You're incredible. Just cause your doorways are low doesn't mean a damn thing, right ? Tom Jones, Richard Burton - all 5'6" but pow, eh? Personal magnetism !

> GARETH. And a hairy chest.

> FREDDIE. Right, right. (sits on the bed rolls a smoke) So, ah, what part of Wales are you from, Gareth ?

> GARETH. Llanllfini. (the "ll"s are pronounced like you're about to spit)

> FREDDIE. Hang on a tick. Say that again and I'll put me raincoat on.
> (laughs)

> GARETH. If you were a galah that'd make you polly-unsaturated.

FREDDIE thinks that's hugely funny.

> FREDDIE. Hey, that's not bad, you want my job? Perhaps you could write my jokes for me. I obviously need some new material.

> GARETH. No thanks. No way. I don't know how you can do that.
> Standing up in front of people, night after night. Just you and the microphone. Jesus, I'd find that really difficult.

> FREDDIE. To be perfectly frank with you, Gareth, I'm finding it pretty difficult myself at the moment. Do you realise I'm officially middle aged.

> GARETH. You don't look a day over 35.

> FREDDIE. (flattered) You know, with make-up I can get it down to 32/33.

GARETH laughs.

> GARETH. That's a gift you've got alright.
>
> FREDDIE (humbly) You think so ? Actually I stole that one from Spike Milligan.
>
> GARETH. You're one of the anointed, Freddie: the fiery preachers, the men who turn words into swords.
>
> FREDDIE. But it's all waffle ultimately. None of it means a damn thing. That's what it's come down to in my game, mate: puns and lavatory humour. There's no *substance* any more, no *guts* to anything. Nobody cares, nobody takes the trouble any more. People are bastards, the world's *stuffed* !
>
> He collapses back onto ROSIE's bed. A man defeated.

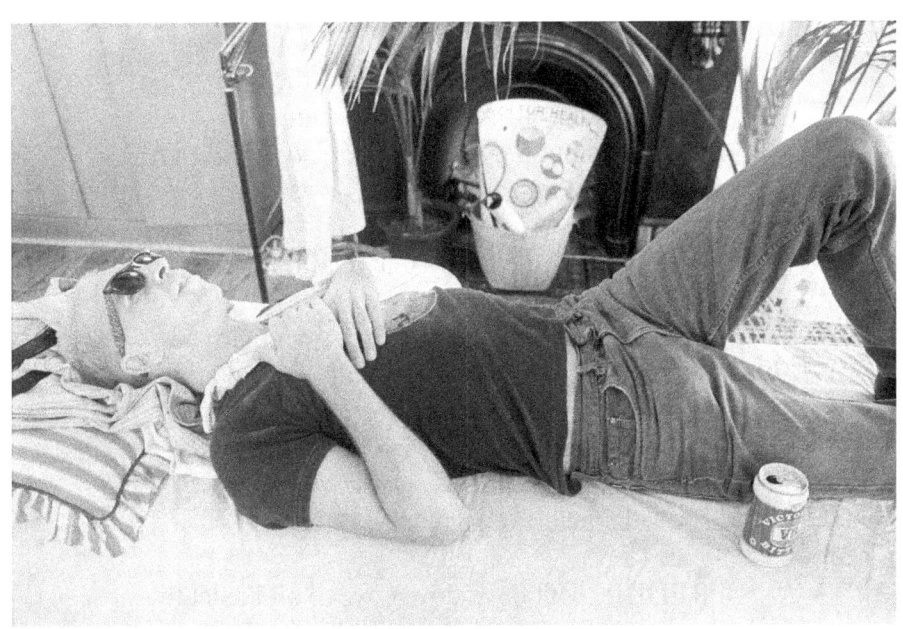

GARETH. Oh, I dunno.

FREDDIE. Why do they steal from you ? Why not pick on someone who can afford it ?

GARETH. I can still shear a sheep. That's my passport. I can still go anywhere outback here and get a job.

FREDDIE. Really ? You can go anywhere ? Now that's what I call a gift, mate. I mean I don't know where I'm going. I haven't got a clue ! Where are we all going ? Eh ? What's it all amount to ?

GARETH. Well, we're all going round the sun about 2 million miles an hour. And the sun's going round a black hole even faster.

FREDDIE. A black hole ! That's it in a nutshell.

GARETH. 'Seems to me you've got to keep your oral traditions intact. That's the only thing they can't steal from you. They can kill individuals but they can't kill *a people* till they smash their language.

FREDDIE. You can say that again.

GARETH. Look at Cymru, my own beloved Wales: 1000 years of Saxon domination and we've still got our culture because we've still got our language. And we've done that *without* national sovereignty. The lesson of Welsh history is the art of survival.

FREDDIE. But deep down, we're all basically the same, aren't we ? People ? Poms, Taffys,

> larrikan Aussies, we've all got a bit of the Celt in us: elusive and indefinable, prone to exaggeration, we all speak in riddles.

GARETH "borrows" the stubbie back off FREDDIE.

> GARETH ... addicted to the use of wine. What about Dylan Thomas, eh ? Language. What about: "Do not go gentle into that good night" ?

GARETH stands and starts declaiming Dylan Thomas and other Welsh poetry in a loud voice, getting louder as he warms to his theme. However, this is interrupted by a sudden, even louder knocking on the door.

> MORREY. (off) Rosie ! *Rosie* !

FREDDIE and GARETH freeze.

> MORREY. (off) Have you got a man in there ?

> FREDDIE. Shit !

> MORREY (off) I know you've got someone, I can hear voices.

> FREDDIE. (to GARETH) Come on !

He frantically bundles GARETH up with his suitcase and together they clamber back out the window just as a key rattles in the door and MORREY sweeps in, still tentative about the gun though, and not quite sure what to expect.

> MORREY. Rosie ?

He feels his way around the room and soon touches upon NICK's neatly folded suit over the back of a chair.

> MORREY. Ah ha ! I thought so.

He bundles the suit under one arm and taps his way over to, and out the window.

> MORREY. *Rosie* ! I've warned you about this.
> You can't hide from me you know.

As soon as he's gone the wardrobe door swings open and NICK tumbles out. He goes to collect his clothes only to discover that they've gone ! He stamps in frustration.

> NICK. Damn !

Out in the corridor SHEILA can he heard CALLING OUT.

> SHEILA. (off) *Where's my perry como record?*

NICK freaks, gathers one of ROSIE's skimpy nighties and nervously throws it on. Suddenly MORRIE reappears at the window

> MORRIE. Ah ha ! I thought so ! (poking his
> cane through the window) You owe me a
> night's accommodation, pal !

MORREY starts climbing back in. NICK switches the light out.

> MORRIE. That doesn't work with me mate.
> That just makes us even.

In the blackness the door swings open and NICK races out, followed by MORREY.

>MORRIE. I want my rent, and I want it now you miserable freeloader! Mary ! Mary!

And MORREY's gone leaving ROSIE's room in darkness again.

A moment later the door swings open and FREDDIE creeps back in, tentative.

>FREDDIE. (whispers) Gareth ?

In the blackout he knocks into something hard on the floor.

>FREDDIE. Geezus !

He picks it up, the light comes on as ROSIE sweeps in and now FREDDIE is caught like a rabbit in the spotlight holding NICK's briefcase.

FREDDIE. (covering his embarrassment with aggression)
What's going on !?

ROSIE. What do you mean "what's going on"
what are you doing
in my room ?

FREDDIE. (shaking the briefcase at her)
What's *he* doing here ?

ROSIE. That's my business.

She snatches the briefcase back from him and drops it out the window.

FREDDIE. I thought you weren't *in* business
anymore.

ROSIE. Look Freddie, you can't begin to
understand what's going on.

FREDDIE. Oh, I know what's going on alright. What's going on is - so much for going cold turkey.

ROSIE. You don't run my life. You don't know the first thing about it.

FREDDIE. Give me a look at your arms.

ROSIE. Get out of it.

FREDDIE. (grabbing for her arms, rolling back the sleeves) Give me a look.

ROSIE. (pulling away from him) *Leave me alone* !

FREDDIE. *Why ? Why ?* Rosie !

ROSIE. Stop *patronising* me !

He picks up NICK's umbrella gesticulating wildly with it.

FREDDIE. You'd done it the hard way. You had it *made* ! Now you're just like all the others no stamina for the long haul. There's no *guts* anymore. This is a Full House alright. A full house of cards ! It used to be a home! It's falling apart in front of us. *You*, you were the one who was supposed to *hold it all together* !

ROSIE takes the brolly off him and also throws it out the window.

ROSIE. Will you calm down.

FREDDIE. (despairing) Rosie, Rosie, Rosie. You had a guy in here ! A customer.

ROSIE. Holding it together is what this is all about. And if you stop carrying on like a prize maniac I might be able to get on with it.

FREDDIE. I just thought, Rosie, I just felt you'd finished with it.

ROSIE. I can't talk now.

FREDDIE. I said I'd support you.

ROSIE. I don't need to be looked after !

FREDDIE. I thought we'd agreed, we were pioneering another way - another way of living together. You, me, Sheila, Mary, Patrick, Dennis - we were a new kind of family because we cared for each other without the old moral codes, marriage and all that shit. It worked because we trusted each other and supported each other. I wanted to support you, Rosie.

ROSIE. On your income ? Don't make me laugh.

FREDDIE. (sadly) Neither you nor anybody else it seems.

ROSIE. Look, Freddie ...

FREDDIE. Alright, I love you, I'm jealous. There, I've said it.

ROSIE. That's silly.

FREDDIE. Why ?

ROSIE. We're friends, that's all. Good friends.

FREDDIE. I lie awake at night thinking about you.

ROSIE. (groans) Look, an old friend of mine has turned up out of the blue tonight - someone I haven't seen for a long time. She needs my help.

FREDDIE. What about me ? Do I count ? I, I need your help tonight, Rosie.

ROSIE. And I need *her*.

FREDDIE. What ? What are you talking... ? Why is everyone talking in riddles these days ? Is that what substitutes for communication now ?

ROSIE. Will you listen to something other than the sound of your own
voice for a change! I'm still ... I feel ... I'm attracted to her that's all.

FREDDIE. (incredulous) A woman ?

ROSIE. We were close friends, it's a female bonding thing.

FREDDIE's hopes fade.

Outside the PHONE can be heard RINGING. (Actually in SHEILA's room).

> FREDDIE. (totally defeated) Alright, then. OK, fine. I mean, flecks of grey are appearing in my beard. I must be past it. Why should an old tree lover and animal liberationist like me expect anything better, eh ?
>
> ROSIE. (the phone) That's probably your agent.
>
> FREDDIE. She can *stuff it* ! I'm through with her as well.
>
> ROSIE. I took a call before, she thinks she's got you a spot on "Hey Hey" with Darryl and Ozzie.

That *is* different.

FREDDIE takes a deep breath. Goes to door, stops.

> FREDDIE. 'Least I always remembered *your* birthday.

And he goes sadly out, summoning as much bruised dignity as he can.

ROSIE decides to head after him.

> ROSIE. (moving out the door) Freddie ! Freddie ! Don't be like that.

As soon as she's gone there's a rattling at the window and MORREY climbs back through, still carrying NICK's suit.

A moment later ROSIE sweeps through the door and pulls up short at the sight of MORREY hanging there.

>ROSIE. Just what the hell do you think you're doing in my room?
>
>MORREY (caught) I'm ... I'm ...
>
>ROSIE. And look at the mess you've made, who's going to clean this up ?
>
>MORREY. What am *I* doing in here ? (shaking the suit at her) What are all these men doing in here
>
>ROSIE. Oh don't you start.

She collapses onto the bed. He looms over her.

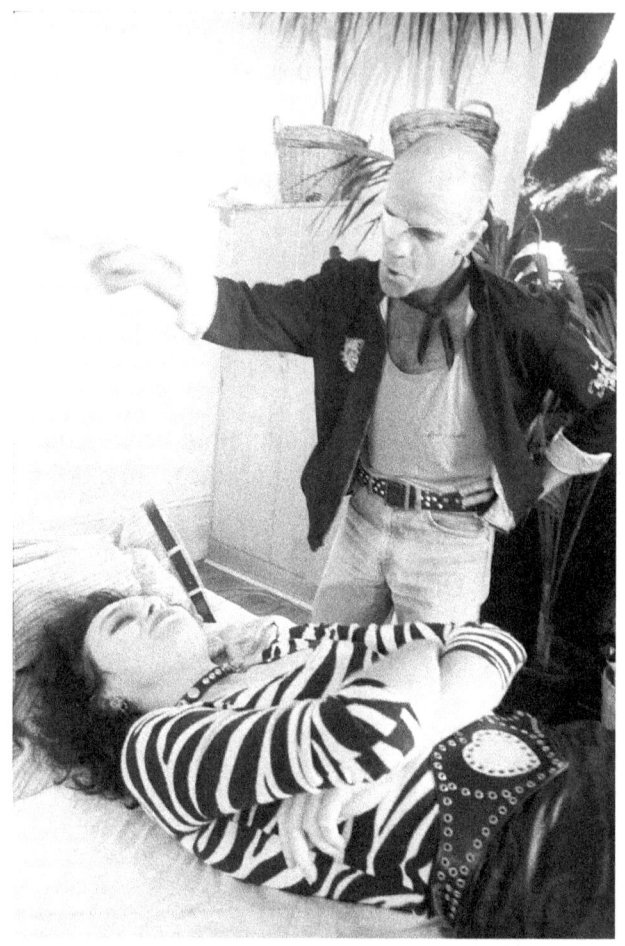

MORREY. There's been more men in here than I could poke a stick at. It's disgusting.

ROSIE. Somebody ought to put hundreds and thousands on your braille, Morrey, and rearrange your furniture.

MORREY. I heard voices, I heard a gun going off in here. Nobody lets guns off in my place.

ROSIE. It's not *your* place.

MORREY. If you have visitors of the opposite sex you're supposed to leave the door open.

ROSIE. There haven't been any men in here except *you*, and bloody Freddie and it's really driving me up the wall. If you're not doing to help me clean this mess up I really wish you'd *piss off*.

MORREY. No men, eh ? Then where did this suit come from ?

ROSIE. (snatching it back) That's my costume for the party.

MORREY taps into a condom on the floor he bends to pick it up.

MORREY. Look at this, look at this ! It's disgusting.

ROSIE. (snatching the condom back) Is that all you think about !

MORREY. I could be closed down if the cops hear about this.

ROSIE. The place *is* closing down anyway.

MORREY. (lowers his voice) You shouldn't spread rumours like that, it upsets the other tenants.

ROSIE. St. Kilda used to have one third of all the rooming houses in Victoria. One third ! Now look what's happening. This is just about the last affordable place left.

MORREY. St. Kilda's been *transformed* in the last few years. It's a paradise compared to what it used to be.

ROSIE. What happens to us, Morrey ? Where do we go now that we can't afford to live here?

MORREY. Why are you so against change? I thought young people were supposed to want it. Isn't that how you put your stamp on things? Out with the old in with the new.

ROSIE. Change for *who*, Morrey ? And into *what* ? The exclusive preserve of the upwardly mobile ? Can't you even see that if St. Kilda loses people like us it loses the kind of social diversity - the very soul of what makes it attractive in the first place ?

MORREY. There's no need to work yourself up into a big lather about it.

ROSIE. (a new thought) They've bought you off, haven't they ?

MORREY. The old joint's got building cancer. Even a blind man can see that it's falling apart.

ROSIE. They've made you an offer to keep the lid on things - smoothe the whole thing through. Stop the residents from agitating too much.

MORREY. Paranoid rubbish !

ROSIE. I'll bet they've even offered you a room in the new place at the same old rent.

MORREY looks a bit sheepish. She can read his discomfort

ROSIE. They have haven't they ?

MORREY. I couldn't interest you in a chook raffle ticket could I ? (he still carries a book of tickets with him)

ROSIE. You traitor, Morrey.

MORREY. Alright, alright it's on the market. But it'll stay a boarding house.

ROSIE. Bullshit.

MORREY. There'll be more flatettes for *more* people.

ROSIE. At a higher price. For those who can afford it.

MORREY. Who wants to live with the likes of Freddie Finally all their lives ? My room could stand some renovation. The place is a dump. If they don't fix it up it will probably fall down.

ROSIE. Is that what they told you ?

MORREY. I've seen the plans.

ROSIE. How can you sell out like this?

MORREY. I'm an invalid pensioner. Who else is going to look after me if I don't look after myself?

ROSIE. What about Sheila?

MORREY. She wants to leave anyway.

ROSIE. So - it's every rat for himself is it? Survival of the greediest.

MORREY. You can't knock it as an evolutionary system. Take a look. It's a mean world out there. Nobody gives a damn.

ROSIE. It's a mean world because we always let the mean bastards ride right over us. They always win because they always divide us off against each other.

MORREY. What's with this "us" and "them" already. They're not unreasonable people. They're saving the goddamn building forcrissake. You could have a room too!

ROSIE. You're the tragedy of a little man, Morrey. You've stuffed it up for all of us.

MORREY. What would you know about it?

ROSIE. I've seen the plans, too, I've seen the hidden agenda. There isn't going to be any renovations, Morrey.

MORREY. I've got assurances.

ROSIE. Which aren't worth the paper they're not written on.

For the first time MORREY looks genuinely concerned.

ROSIE. I've just been with some agents.

MORREY. Agents !

ROSIE. Real estate agents. I overheard them bragging about this place at Cafe Minimalist. Fortunately for us I've managed to pick one of them up.

MORREY. So you *did* have a man in here.!

ROSIE. Yes, and I've got a plan and you've got a chance to redeem yourself by helping me blackmail him.

ROSIE gives MORREY a polaroid camera that she's brought in from LIZ's room.

MORREY. I can't do this.

Next, ROSIE pulls a contract from inside NICK's suit coat, opens it and shows it to MORREY.

ROSIE. Then read between the lines for a change.

MORREY lifts his sunglasses, puts his broken binocular lens to his one "good" eye and skims through the document.

MORREY. A wedding reception centre and car park ! They're pulling it all down for a carpark ?

ROSIE. A multi-storey carpark.

MORREY. They can't do that, this building is classified.

ROSIE. Oh they'll keep the facade. But they need the car spaces so they can get a liquor licence That's why they've bought *Linga Longa*, and why they've conned you into keeping the peasants ignorant.

MORREY. I've never been evicted from anywhere in my life.

ROSIE. Get used to it, Morrey, or get used to this camera.

MORREY. But I'm on a disability pension. I'm a protected tenant.

ROSIE. That doesn't apply if there's no longer any residence to rent in.

MORREY. What can we do?

ROSIE. (indicating some of the mess on the floor) Get me that dog collar and the handcuffs.

ROSIE drops a pile of pills in a glass of scotch.

ROSIE. If we can discredit this guy and threaten him with the Vice Squad they'll never get a liquor licence and without that, the idea of wedding receptions just won't make economic sense.

MORREY. You're not going to do anything illegal are you?

ROSIE bundles MORREY and camera under the bed.

ROSIE. Wait under there till I call you.

MORREY. But, but Rosie. .

ROSIE. Shh!

LIZ'S SCREAM can be heard off.

MORREY re-emerges from under the bed at the sound of LIZ screaming.

MORREY. What was that?!

ROSIE takes out a blow-up doll from one of her drawers and shoves it at MORREY, pushing him back under the bed.

ROSIE. Blow that up. Quickly !

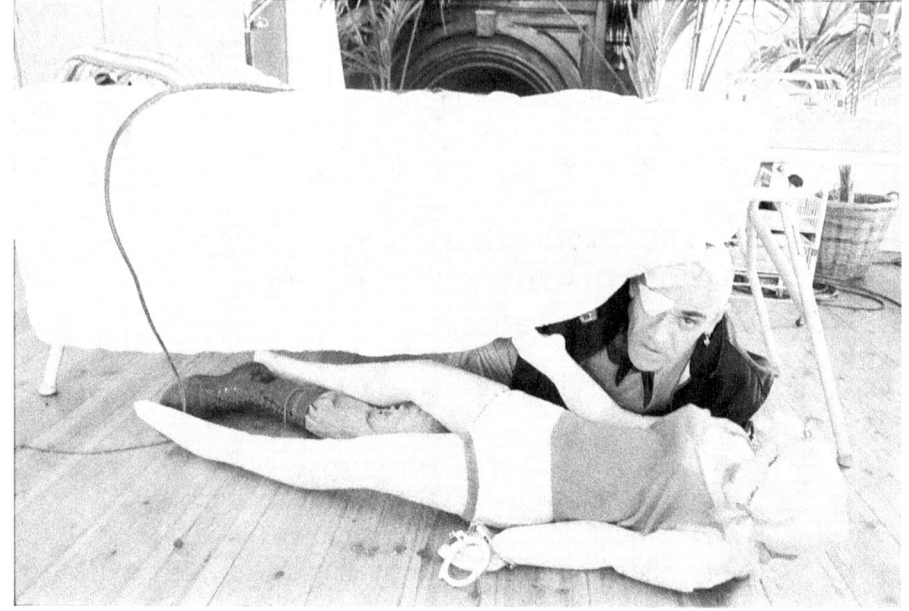

MORREY What ?

ROSIE. Hide hide !

A moment later NICK scrambles in through the window. He's retrieved his briefcase and umbrella from where ROSIE dropped them.

ROSIE turns on him angry.

ROSIE. Where the hell have you been !

NICK. Where have I been !? I've been tearing all over the place feeling like a prize twerp. I mean- look at me ! What have you done to me ?

All he wears still is the skimpy dressing gown.

ROSIE. (smooth sexy voice) Don't worry about that now. Let's relax, put our feet up.

He snatches his suit back, quickly throws it back on.

>NICK. You can put your feet where you like. I'm putting mine out the doorway.

>ROSIE. You don't have to race off, do you ?

>NICK. I can't wait to get out of the place.

>ROSIE. I'm sorry to hear that.

>NICK. It's the most embarrassing nightcap I've never had. Where are my shoes ?!

>ROSIE. (looking around) Oh ah …

They suddenly appear behind NICK (MORREY sliding them out from under the bed). ROSIE's eyes widen but she tries not to give anything away.

>ROSIE. There they are !

As he bends down to pick them up an arm of the doll falls out from under the other end of the bed. NICK reacts, alarmed.

>NICK. What was that !

>ROSIE. Nothing.

>NICK. Nothing ?!

>ROSIE. Just one of my props, nothing important. (kicking it back under the bed)

>NICK. This place is wierd.

>ROSIE. (holding the scotch bottle) You can't go without one drink, surely. I promised you that much.

NICK. No, thank you.

ROSIE. But now I feel awful.

NICK. I think I've had enough excitement for one night.

ROSIE. You're going to miss our little Happy Hour.

NICK. You can't have everything.

ROSIE. Well, I'm sorry to see you rush off like this.

NICK. The pleasure is entirely mine.

Sadly she watches him complete his dressing. Having got it all back on NICK feels more secure. Relaxes for a moment.

Now the doll's leg appears from under the bed. ROSIE looks as if she could kill MORREY. But NICK doesn't see it. ROSIE composes herself.

ROSIE. Back to normal.

NICK. Yeah.

She holds his look with a beguiling, sad smile.

ROSIE. Well, no point wasting it. (pours herself a scotch)

He hangs there a moment, feeling a touch guilty.

NICK. (looking around the room) You've got some pretty strange props.

ROSIE. Oh they're just something I collect.

NICK. Must've cost a bit.

ROSIE. All tax deductible. Business expenses.

NICK Smart.

He holds out his hand.

NICK. Well, good-night. Can't say I really enjoyed it.

ROSIE. Perhaps another time.

NICK. I don't think so.

As she shakes hands with him she frowns, feels his forearm.

ROSIE. (concerned) God you're tense.

She works her hand up towards his shoulder.

ROSIE. You're so tight up there.

NICK. (shrugs) Pressure of work.

ROSIE. What do you do ? Strangle people ?

NICK. (smirks) Bit of this and that.

ROSIE. You should relax more. Cut the worry. You'll bring on something terminal. (she continues to rub his shoulders)

NICK. Hah! Solve all my problems.

ROSIE. No job's worth dying for.

NICK. It's not just the job. It's ...

ROSIE. Some *one* ? A lover ?

He nods.

>NICK. Tonight would've been our 3rd anniversary.
>
>ROSIE. You split up ?
>
>NICK. She left me 8 months ago. Not so much as a note. Not even a single line since then.
>
>ROSIE. That's tough.
>
>NICK. She's the only girl I ever asked to marry me. And I still would if I could find her. I fully intended to drink myself into oblivion tonight. I'm so depressed I could kill myself.

He collapses onto her bed again. She descends with him, keeping up the massage...

>ROSIE. That's stupid.

NICK. Yeah.

ROSIE keeps rubbing, having worked her way round the back and is now concentrating on both shoulders.

>NICK. (closing his eyes) Oh, that ... that feels *so* good.

He collapses back onto the bed. She works on his legs.

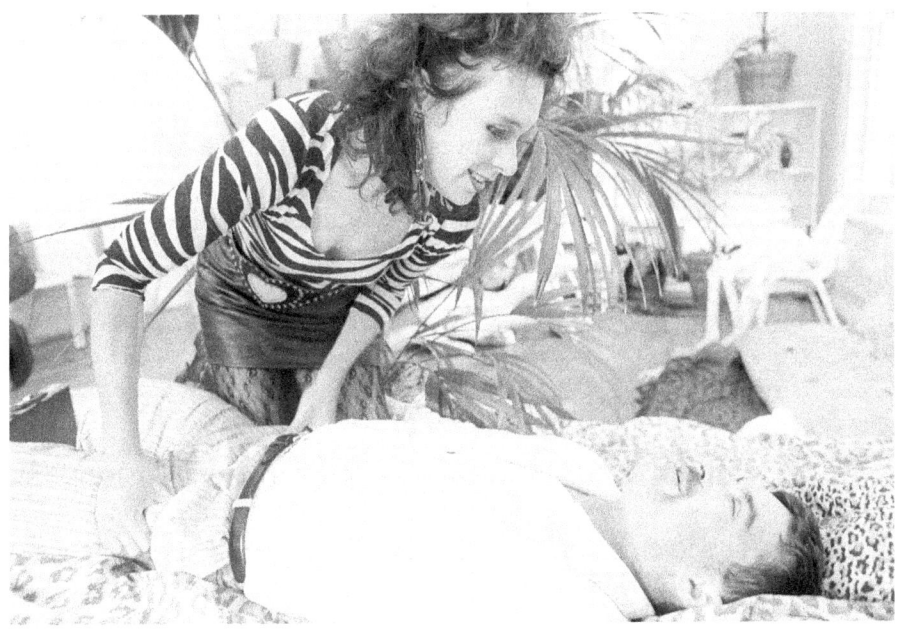

>ROSIE. Are you sure you won't have just one nightcap ?

>NICK. (pleasured out) Hmm ?

She works him like a pro. He's soon putty in her hands.

>ROSIE. (enticing, girly voice) Just one for the road ?

>NICK. (stretching his neck) God that's so nice. Where did you learn to do that ?

ROSIE. Would you like some ice ?

As she works him with one hand she turns to pick up the drugged glass of scotch but having poured one for herself she's not sure which is which. She takes a punt, moves the glass to his hand which automatically takes it. She continues to rub with both hands.

NICK. Oh thanks - that's so … fiiiinnnnne.

She finds a particularly vulnerable spot.

NICK. Yes, there ! Oh that's the spot.

He idly sips the scotch, closes his eyes again, luxuriating in the massage.

ROSIE. How about there - (finding another spot)

NICK. Mmm Mmm.

He takes a few more sips.

NICK. Your hands are great, so ... so strong.

He finishes the scotch in one gulp. She eases off the rubbing. Anxious to see if it's actually the right glass.

NICK. (grabbing her hand) Don't stop.

ROSIE. (backing off a little) What ?

Still holding her he pulls himself to his feet and stands, facing her.

ROSIE. (innocently) What's going on ?

NICK. Why don't you rub me all over with oil ?

ROSIE. I don't have any oil.

NICK. I thought that's what you went to get. To oil your hands...

ROSIE tries to disengage from his grip. But NICK holds on, his manner becomes suddenly vicious again.

ROSIE. I think you've got the wrong idea.

NICK. (leering at her) Come on darling, the props, the bed that doubles as a massage table. That's what it's all about isn't it ?

ROSIE. I invited you home for a drink.

NICK. So we've had that, now let's get down to business.

ROSIE. I thought you wanted to go.

NICK. Come on, you practically dragged me in here. (suddenly vicious) You tart !

He goes to make a final lunge at her, embracing her roughly, she SCREAMS, fighting back

ROSIE. No ! Please No ! Let go ! Morrey ! Morrey !

MORREY scrambles back out from under the bed and quickly fires off a polaroid shot of NICK.

NICK watches this as if in a dream, he turns to ROSIE and looks about to strangle her but his lunge forward turns into a fall as he drops into her arms unconscious.

Still holding NICK upright she rips the polaroid snap ejected from the camera and tears it up.

MORREY What ?

ROSIE. Not me, him, by himself, God, Morrey, wake up.

MORREY. Sorry.

ROSIE. Alright, get the doll, put it on the bed.

As MORREY does so ROSIE rotates NICK puts a dog collar around his neck and a whip in the other hand. She positions him above the doll, lifts the whip hand.

ROSIE. Right now, shoot, MORREY, shoot !

Just before MORREY bangs off another shot ROSIE drops out of sight. NICK slumps across the doll, like a puppet that's just had it's strings cut.

ROSIE. Are you getting the doll in ?

MORREY. How would I know ? I'm legally blind.

With great difficulty she lifts NICK off the doll and raises his arm.

ROSIE. Take another one then.

Again MORREY bangs off another shot as ROSIE disappears. behind NICK. ROSIE repeats the procedure a third time.

ROSIE. One for safety.

MORREY fires again.

MORREY. One for the album.

ROSIE. Don t be sick, MORREY, that's enough. Now let's get him out of here. Dump him in the gutter. Let him wake up where he belongs.

With some difficulty MORREY and ROSIE gather NICK by the arms and drop him onto a small rug which they then use to drag him out the door.

1930s/40s DANCE MUSIC from the start of the Happy Hour can be heard wafting in from the Dining Room out the back.

FREDDIE'S ROOM

FREDDIE's room is a mess, there's a month's worth of dirty laundry piled in a heap on the floor next to the bed which is an unmade mattress stuck on top of a number of milk crates. The wardrobe has been improvised out of two stacks of wooden boxes with a piece of dowling running between them to hang clothes off. Over on a small table is a frypan, an electric jug and stack of dirty plates in a large plastic bowl. Around the walls are numerous posters of FREDDIE in his stand-up costumes - indicating that he's appeared at comedy gigs in various pubs around Melbourne. There's also a small library of books stacked in piles as well as heaps of cardboard boxes with bits of newspapers and other memorabilia stuffed into them.

A fuzzy, portable black and white TV is on and has been vaguely audible in the other rooms.

Out in the Hallway a CLOCK CHIMES 8.15.

The door opens and LIZ enters. She carries a heavy backpack and a large white suitcase identical to the one we saw GARETH with. She is also about 8 and a half months pregnant.

She pauses near the door to survey the room, it's certainly nothing to write home about. And she seems tentative, not sure of her ground. However she mercifully turns the sound on the TV down.

She comes forward, drops her suitcase, unloads the backpack and goes to survey the view through the window pulling back a cheap calico curtain. All she can see is other nondescript brick flats. So she lets the curtain fall closed and turns back to the room, fiddling with a ring on her wedding finger - twisting it self-consciously.

She returns to the backpack, slips a copy of "Asia On $10 A Day" from out of one of the side flaps, considers the book for a moment, then drops it in the bin (an old paint tin).

She turns to a small laminex table (FREDDIE's "desk"). She rubs a finger along it. It's pretty dirty so she wipes it clean and sits in front of it. She finally takes the "wedding" ring off and places it carefully down on the table in front of her.

From this position she is able to lean over and take out from another side flap in her back pack a small writing pad, biro, and a photo of herself and a young man mounted on card - something that's obviously been taken at a restaurant somewhere, some years ago.(We might recognise that it's NICK from the previous scene. She sets the card up in front of her and is just about to write something when.

A GUNSHOT IS HEARD OFF.

Startled, LIZ springs to her feet, glancing anxiously at the door, expecting godknows what to come through it.

After a moment - SILENCE. No other sound of alarm.

So she relaxes a little, pulls out a cigarette and lights it, but almost immediately she stubs it out in the broken down fire place. She considers for a moment then throws the rest of the cigarette pack into the fireplace for good measure. She's made a decision about smoking and she's going to stick to it.

She feels her pregnant belly, smiles the little, and resumes her seat in front of the letter pad.

> LIZ. (out loud as she writes) Dear NICK, I'm writing this now but I don't even know for sure where you live. I guess I'll try the phone book - or your mother - if she'll still talk to me. There are many things to tell you, above all one big surprise, and I know you won't believe me, but I've tried to start this letter many times in the past 8 months. It just never seemed to come out right. You must be hurt I know, by the way in

> which I left and then kept on going. But as you'll see from the post mark I'm finally back in the land of Oz to claim a traveller's inheritance: the single woman with her single bed in her (looks round) borrowed single room. That says it all don't you think ? But then what do we need of beds or houses or anything else. You can't take it with you, and besides, nobody lives forever...

She glances over what she's written, sighs, tears it slowly and neatly in two and drops it in the bin on top of the travel book. Then she props her head in her hands and leans forward on the table.

From this position she glances across at her suitcase, goes over to it. Undoes the catches on it to unpack something, then has a second thought, closes it again, grabs the back pack, the photo and is about to leave again when there's a knock on the door.

LIZ freezes. Drops the bags, scrambles to retrieve the ring (she was going to leave it behind) and slips it back on her wedding finger.

> ROSIE (off) Hullo ? Liz ?

ROSIE's voice relaxes her.

> ROSIE. (off) Are you decent ?

ROSIE pokes her head around the door, smiling.

ROSIE. Welcome back stranger.

LIZ. Rosie!

ROSIE enters, hugs her, careful of the baby.

ROSIE. You were away too long.

LIZ. I know, I know. .

ROSIE. Let me look at you.

ROSIE disengages but still holds LIZ by the hands, standing back from her.

ROSIE. You look fantastic.

LIZ. (coy) I don't.

ROSIE. You do, Lizzie, it's motherhood, that's what it is. You look gorgeous.

LIZ. Stop it.

ROSIE. You are, you're remarkable.

LIZ. I'm thin. Too thin.

ROSIE. You've always been thin.

LIZ. Not when you're having a monster like this. It's a bit of a worry.

ROSIE. You look great. I'm so proud of you deciding to follow it through. Falling pregnant, going it alone. It's marvellous.

LIZ. Funny expression "*falling* pregnant" like you've tripped over or something. Fallen down a hole.

ROSIE. You'll be fine. You're home now. That's the main thing.

LIZ. Home ? Oh no, Rosie, I couldn't impose on you like that.

ROSIE. You're staying with me and that's an end to it. Just consider yourself a permanent resident of one of the last of the genuine St. Kilda boarding houses.

LIZ. I thought I heard a gunshot.

ROSIE. Probably just Morrey shooting another trespasser.

LIZ. (shocked) You're not serious

ROSIE. (smiles) Oh there aren't as many gunshots or sirens as there used to be. Actually, I miss the sirens. They kind of reassure you that there's someone out there you can still rely on.

LIZ. I can't believe you've finally settled down.

ROSIE. Three years in this very house, that's a personal record.

LIZ. And you're happy here ?

ROSIE. Oh I'll never leave St. Kilda. It's funny for a country girl to say this, but I feel like I've finally come home.

LIZ. I don't think I could ever get attached to the one place again.

ROSIE. Where in all the world could you find that walk along the upper Esplanade ? The pleasure domes, the palm trees, the horizon - it calms the soul.

LIZ. When you can see it through the pollution.

ROSIE. Elizabeth O'Brien, professional cynic.

LIZ. I'm a pessioptimist who's finally decided that the world looks all the same from 39,000 feet.

ROSIE. Fine, if you're going to be an airhostess.

LIZ. That's what I like about travelling, it gets you out of yourself. Keeps you from brooding about unimportant things like what you're actually doing with your life.

ROSIE. What is it ? Two? Two and a half years ? Since I've seen you ?

LIZ. More like three I think.

ROSIE. God is it really ? You must tell me all about it. Everything, I want photographs, dates, places.

LIZ. It'll be very boring.

ROSIE. As soon as you've settled.

LIZ. Rosie, I can't impose on you like this.

ROSIE. Look - I'm sorry about having to divert you in here for the moment. We'll fix you up in my room as soon as I can get rid of this guy.

LIZ. I don't want to be any trouble.

ROSIE. Believe me, this is one eviction I'm really looking forward to.

LIZ. It'll only be for one night.

ROSIE. Don't be silly, you're *staying* with me.

LIZ. No I couldn't really.

ROSIE. My dear it's all settled. As soon as the baby comes you can move upstairs, there's a flatette vacant on the twenty first.

LIZ. I can't afford it Rosie. Not here.

ROSIE. Don't worry about that now. You'll get your single mother's pension when the child is born. Plus, I've got a little nest egg tucked away. That should get us through the hospital part of it. I know someone with a cot and I'm pretty sure (we can hit them for a pram as well…

LIZ. (cutting in) Rosie, please, you're very kind but I...

ROSIE. I *want* to do it Lizzie, it will give me great pleasure to do it.

LIZ looks down, close to tears. ROSIE comes forward, puts an arm around her.

ROSIE. You know I love you.

LIZ kisses her on the cheek and disengages. ROSIE watches her open the top of her backpack, take out a small elastic indoor clothes line, pegs, and a plastic bag full of wet clothes.

LIZ. (as she puts up the line) I've been trying to get these dry since Phuket 3 days ago.

ROSIE helps her peg up some smalls.

ROSIE. Don't suppose anybody will invent a less labour intensive way of hanging out the washing.

LIZ. No.

ROSIE. (taking in the two bags) Is this all you've got?

LIZ. All I've got in the world.

ROSIE. That's very impressive, Lizzie, I mean for a cynic, you've got some discipline, I'll give you that much.

LIZ. I must admit it was difficult to avoid splurging out in Italy, but by then I was living off bankcards anyway.

ROSIE. I thought there had to be a pragmatic reason for your sudden return.

LIZ. Oh, I'm worse than broke. I'm probably actually technically bankrupt. But in a funny way, I couldn't care less. Coming here in the bus from Tullamarine I felt so ridiculously important. I just got this feeling all of a sudden that Australia is so precious and so lucky and time is very short and there's a thousand things I want to do. A million things to photograph.

ROSIE. A baby'll soon knock that rubbish out of you.

LIZ smiles.

ROSIE. What about the father?

LIZ. (shrugs) I dunno...

ROSIE. Don't know where he is ?

LIZ. Don't know *who* he is.

ROSIE. Oh Lizzie !

LIZ. Well, it's hard to be sure. I had this guy - Nick. You never met him. It was after the Brunswick house. Eight and a half months ago we had a big fight and I left. I walked straight out and did a really crazy thing I bought a ticket to Europe and was in Paris the next day. That was all the money I had saved from 2 years of emergency nursing.

ROSIE. Well - you should tell him, this Nick. Surely he has a right to know.

LIZ. Trouble is, I met a French boy almost straight away.

ROSIE. Oh Lizzie !

LIZ. It could be either of them.

ROSIE. Oh God !

LIZ. No, Mitch, was great - Michel - he was a friend. He was there when I needed someone. 'Took me to Amersterdam. Of course it only lasted 3 weeks but I was grateful for Amsterdam. That's where I linked up with a couple of Canadians and came back to Asia. I even started nursing again.

She retrieves her packet of discarded cigarettes from the fireplace, lights one.

LIZ. In Goa this big Swiss company had dumped a whole lot of powdered milk on the market - inducing young mother's to buy it when their own breast milk was fine. Of course the mother's were mixing the powder with unsterilised water. As a result hundreds, maybe thousands of babies died. No one was charged. They didn't even stop dumping the stuff. After that I decided to come home. (looks at the cigarette)
God, why am I doing this ? (stubs it out) I was down to three a day.

ROSIE. I still think you should tell him.

LIZ. Nick ?

ROSIE. Well, it *may* be his.

LIZ. That's a good name for a girl, don't you think, May ?

ROSIE. Stop avoiding the issue.

LIZ. Nick and I had only one thing in common - we were going to get married on the same day. Then we had two things in common. He didn't like me and I hated him.

ROSIE. It can't be that bad.

LIZ. He's a quantity surveyor with investments in property! That's why I had to stop nursing. He needed me at home to do the entertaining.

ROSIE. Behind every great woman there's a great man. .

LIZ. Who tried to stop her.

They share a smile.

LIZ. He never had money to start with, I'll give him that much, now he's the sort of bloke who'll leave his porsche in a disabled parking spot without blinking an eyelid.

ROSIE. I could never understand careers, that sheep-like dedication to doing one thing all your life. It implies a certain mental abberation if you ask me.

LIZ. Oh come on, I remember you at college. You were going to start a magazine that would finally destroy the Women's Weekly.

ROSIE. And here we are, ten years later - I'm on the dole and you've got nowhere to live.

LIZ. Charming but alarming.

ROSIE. What about your family ?

LIZ. I couldn't go back to Stanthorpe. A single mother would really stuff up their social image. Besides, my brothers are still fighting over Dad's estate.

ROSIE. Where there's a Will there's a family feud.

LIZ. Anyway, that's my story, what about you ?

ROSIE. Me ?

LIZ. As usual you've managed to avoid talking about yourself.

ROSIE. There's nothing to add your honour.

LIZ. Nothing, to add, I haven't *heard* anything yet.

ROSIE. Me ? I'm the classic example of the only truly postmodern tragedy: a woman who finally realised she wanted a child only at that point where it's virtually too late to do so.

LIZ. You're not that old.

ROSIE. I'm nearly that old darling and it takes two to tango.

LIZ. So ?

ROSIE. So where am I going to find a guy at this stage?

LIZ. Rosie, you're beautiful, you'll have no trouble at all.

> ROSIE. I'm afraid the gene pool represented by the males around here leaves a lot to be desired.
>
> LIZ. So - that's why you need to travel.
>
> ROSIE. I don't like travel, I like coming home to the news every night. Anyway I don't *need* to travel, I'm living in the most fabulous city in the world.
>
> LIZ. What you *need* is someone like Mitch.
>
> ROSIE. Darling, my life has reached a plateau of idyllic calm. I'm entering a serene, early middle age without complications.
>
> LIZ. I've got a photograph of him somewhere. .

She goes to open her suitcase...

> LIZ. Oh no !
>
> ROSIE. What ?

LIZ holds up a man's shaving kit, pulling it out of the suitcase.

> LIZ. Can you believe this !? What is it with me and goddam planes? Something always goes wrong.

ROSIE picks up some more items from the suitcase - obviously male clothing.

> ROSIE. Nice trousers - you sure you want to take it back ?

LIZ. This isn't funny, all my photos were in there, eight months worth !

ROSIE puts the trousers down and takes out a polaroid camera. Studies it.

ROSIE. Well, you've gained a camera.

LIZ. Oh god !

ROSIE. You know, I've just had a brilliant idea.

LIZ. What ?

ROSIE rummages through the suitcase and finds some film.

ROSIE. (holding the polaroid and the film) Blackmail.

LIZ looks quizzical.

ROSIE. If you don't fight you lose.

LIZ. Come again ?

ROSIE. This could solve all our problems. I'll explain it to you later. Meet me in the Dining Room in ten minutes.

But before LIZ can ask another question ROSIE is gone with the camera.

LIZ turns back to the "foreign" suitcase. Checks a few items: a Welsh national flag, a pair of pyjamas, a priest's collar, a copy of "Australia on $25 a Day", a stethoscope, a seacaptain's hat- a wealth of costumes - or disguises...

She frowns at the stuff just as we hear SHEILA calling out.

SHEILA (off) *Where's my perry como record !!??*

A moment later SHEILA barges in.

> SHEILA Morrey ?...

SHEILA spots LIZ, pulls up short. Obviously she was expecting to find MORREY.

> SHEILA. Oh - I beg your pardon.
>
> LIZ. (not sure of her own ground) That's alright.
>
> SHEILA. I was just looking for Morrey.
>
> LIZ. Yes.
>
> SHEILA. Didn't realise Freddie had a ... visitor.
>
> LIZ. Freddie ?

SHEILA notices the washing hanging on LIZ's improvised line.

> SHEILA. He should've told you there's a laundromat round in Grey Street.
>
> LIZ. Oh - it's ... simpler this way, just a few things.
>
> SHEILA. Still it is a bit squashed in here- especially for two of ... er three of you.
>
> LIZ. What
>
> SHEILA. (covering her embarrassment) Er - I've got the front room, the one with the bay windows.
>
> LIZ. That's nice.

SHEILA. Would've had a view of the sea once... before the land boom put that horrible big gothic Victorian place across the road.

LIZ. Yes.

SHEILA. But that was a long time ago...

There's an awkward pause, LIZ doesn't know quite what to say.

SHEILA. Look, I suppose we'd better get to know each other if we're going to be neighbours. I'm Sheila, Sheila Dwyer.

LIZ. Hullo, Liz O'Brien.

They shake hands.

SHEILA. I must say Freddie certainly kept you under wraps.

LIZ. Look, I think you misunder...(stand).

SHEILA. Still. it's nice to see him finally settling down with someone, taking a few responsibilities for a change. Be sure you keep him in line though. He's a devil of a bloke at the best of times.

LIZ. Actually I ...

But SHEILA rattles on.

SHEILA. I expect Freddie's told you about me. I'm in the business too, of course.

LIZ. No.

SHEILA. (disappointed) He hasn't ?

LIZ. Well, ahm, no, I'm not staying ...

SHEILA takes in the baby.

SHEILA. Not staying ?

She looks concerned.

LIZ. No ah, I'm just passing through.

SHEILA. He can't possibly let you "just past through" it's not honourable. I *insist* that you stay. That boy's got to wake up to himself, especially now that it's out in the open. .

LIZ. Look I don't know this Freddie chap from a bar of soap.

SHEILA looks doubly shocked.

SHEILA Well, I must say. You young lot, you're hard to figure. I know it's been open slather since the 1960s, but I do think you should consider the child. I mean, OK a fling on the side, everybody's done it but there comes a point when you go this far ... Every child needs a father even if the parents don't ... don't know each other.

LIZ. I'm sorry- I'm just waiting here for Rosie.

SHEILA. You're not with Freddie ?

LIZ. No - I'm literally ... I'm just borrowing his room.

SHEILA. (realises) Oh- you're Rosie's friend. Oh I do apologise. Silly me. What a silly duffer I am. I thought you were ... Yes. I remember now. Rosie said you were coming. You're the little Queenslander.

LIZ. I grew up in Queensland ... haven't been back there for a while.

SHEILA. Well, welcome to the Linga Longa, darling.

LIZ. Thank you.

SHEILA. We're a pretty friendly bunch here. One big happy family really- except for Morrey. But don't let him worry you.. Beneath that grumpy exterior there beats a heart of lead.

LIZ. I don't know if I'll be staying all that long.

SHEILA. Oh nonsense. After a few days you won't be able to leave the place - except to go to the hospital of course (chuckles) It'll be marvellous to have a child around here again. What's a home without children.

LIZ. A house ?

SHEILA. Exactly. I hope you're coming to our Happy Hour ?

LIZ. Well, actually I'm (feeling a little weary)...

SHEILA. I've got this fantastic arab costume you must wear. It'll ... (indicating the belly) cover you, you know. And forget Freddie, you might meet the love of your life.

LIZ. Really I...

SHEILA. I'll get it for you straight away.

The phone can be heard RINGING in SHEILA'S room. SHEILA reacts, delighted.

> SHEILA. The agency ! (to LIZ) Don't go away.

And she bounces out to answer the phone. As soon as SHEILA's gone LIZ moves over and tries on the Queen of Sheba head-dress that she's left behind. She checks the fit in a small cracked mirror just as FREDDIE blusters in. There's mutual shock. They hold each other's look for a moment.

> FREDDIE. Excuse me, I'll just try that again.

FREDDIE goes back outside, closes the door knocks.

> FREDDIE. (off) Knock knock.

> LIZ. Who's there ?

> FREDDIE. (off) Isobel.

> LIZ. Isobel who ?

> FREDDIE. (poking his head round the door) Is the bell working ? I've been knocking for hours.

FREDDIE laughs heartily at his own joke. Comes fully into the room.

> FREDDIE. No, seriously - knock, knock.

> LIZ. Who's there ?

> FREDDIE. Ah, you've heard that one.

Again he nearly kills himself laughing at his own joke.

> LIZ. (not amused) Are you right ?

FREDDIE. No, I'm left actually. Have been ever since Vietnam.

LIZ. (a little more sternly, impatient) Can I help you?

FREDDIE. I hope so, I'm looking for a thongathon player to accompany my solo guitar.

LIZ. Look, this is a private room.

FREDDIE. (taking in the clothes) Looks more like a Chinese laundry.

LIZ. I'm sorry, but I'm going to have to ask you to leave.

She remains firmly on her side of the room. The line of washing that she's hung up (about chest height) effectively hides the fact that she's pregnant from FREDDIE. He thinks he's onto a good thing. He puts some music on his battered cassette player. (Bolero)

LIZ. (concerned) What are you doing?

FREDDIE. I find Ravel tremendously exciting don't you?

LIZ. Are you listening to me?

FREDDIE. Full of guts and substance and hot spanish blood! Incredibly erotic.

LIZ. (alarmed) Erotic?

FREDDIE. Women can't resist it, I find I … usually get what I want by the seventh movement… (advancing on her)

LIZ. You're pretty sure of yourself.

> FREDDIE. I ought to be.
>
> LIZ. Why's that ?
>
> FREDDIE. Well - this is my room.

LIZ wishes the ground would swallow her.

> LIZ. Oh- I'm, I'm terribly sorry.
>
> FREDDIE. That's alright, make yourself at home. Pull up a chair, help yourself to some cake, catch up on your washing ... Don't mind me I only live here.
>
> LIZ. I must apologise, I didn't know, Rosie you see ...
>
> FREDDIE. Rosie ?
>
> LIZ. It's the first chance I've had to air them. (starts to dismantle her washing line)
>
> FREDDIE. Please - be my guest. It's not everyday I come home to find a beautiful Mary Magdalen waiting to tempt me.

LIZ had forgotten about the Arabian head-dress. She whips it off.

> FREDDIE. (again the Casanova act, moving in on her) Here comes the seventh movement...

But he reaches LIZ just as she takes the line away - revealing her pregnancy to him for the first time. FREDDIE stops dead in his tracks. His eyes boggle.

FREDDIE. *Ohmygod*! You're incredibly *pregnant* ! Oh- er (gulp) congratualitons. (an afterthought) I hope…

He switches off the music.

FREDDIE. Oh, Christ ! Oh god ! How gauche of me. Now I feel awful.

LIZ. Well, it's mutual then.

FREDDIE. That was unforgiveable.

LIZ. I don't see what difference being pregnant makes.

FREDDIE. (fumbling) No, well, of course, but … anyway now that I've made a complete dickhead of myself I'd better say I'm Freddie Finally.

He holds out his hand. She holds out hers. But instead of shaking it he jumps his hand back and forth over hers.

FREDDIE. President of the Ping Pond association.

She smiles. He helps her pack up the rest of her washing.

FREDDIE. Oh, look, you've got a hole in your sock. (holding it up)

LIZ. (grabbing it back) I have not.

FREDDIE. Yes you have.

LIZ No.

FREDDIE. Then how do you get your foot in ?

LIZ. You should be on the stage.

FREDDIE. Yeah, the next one out of town.

LIZ. Are all your jokes that old ?

FREDDIE. Only the really funny ones. (slight pause) Actually, I *am* on the stage.

LIZ. You're a professional then ?

FREDDIE. In a manner of speaking.

LIZ. What do you do ? Professionally ?

FREDDIE. I worry. I worry a lot. And eventually this worrying will kill me. So I worry about that. My mother tried to put me off a theatrical career by burning all my early plays. I could've been something really sensible like a dentist or a computer programmer. Now look at me, a clown prince with $27.50 in the bank.

LIZ. I've never understood that artist-in-a-garret stuff. You shouldn't be in a garret. You should shout your ideas from the rooftops.

FREDDIE. Oh I've tried rooftops but a) the box office is lousy, b) I usually end up in gaol and c) next week I'll probably be living there. Speaking of which - where are you ah...

LIZ. Here I think.

FREDDIE. Here ?

LIZ. The *Linga Longa*.

FREDDIE. But it's full, the house is full, there are no vacancies.

LIZ. With Rosie.

FREDDIE. Right, right, you're Rosie's friend. Oh, well, I don't think Morrey'd ever let you do that. He's very strict about sharing.

LIZ. They said I could have the upstairs room- from the 20th.

FREDDIE. What ? I've been waiting for that room for six months !

LIZ. Oh - I'm sorry, I didn't ... they said it's available, that's all.

FREDDIE. It's the only reason I agreed to stick it out in this black hole in the first place. Morrey promised me that room.

LIZ. Well, I'll take your room then.

FREDDIE. Oh I don't think you'd want to live here, really. It'd be a terrible place to bring up a kid, full of drunks and drug addicts and screams in the night.

LIZ. I've stayed in worse places.

FREDDIE. You, yes, but think of the child ! I mean, god, we had such happy childhoods compared to the kids today. I even won a smiling competition when I was five. That's how I started in this business. One pound for simply smiling at a picture theatre full of kids. You know what a pound could buy in 1956 ? A dozen bottles of Sarsaparilla ! That was the sort of environment to bring a kid up in. And really, a smile was dead easy in those days. You see that - that ?

He bungs on a deliberate smile for her.

>FREDDIE. That's a champion smile.

It looks ghastly.

>FREDDIE. (still smiling) Give us a look at yours.
>
>LIZ. 'Afraid I don't have much to smile about.
>
>FREDDIE. Oh go on, it won't crack your face.

LIZ clutches her stomache, is wracked by convulsions, looks like she's about to throw up.

>FREDDIE. Oh - oh god are you alright?
>
>LIZ. (breathing hard) Yeah- sort of …
>
>FREDDIE. It's not coming is it ? Should I put the kettle on ? Tear up some sheets?
>
>LIZ. It's alright.
>
>FREDDIE. Oh Jesus !
>
>LIZ. It's just this really bad diahorrea I picked up in Bangkok.

Clutching her stomach, she races out the door.

>FREDDIE. Oh this is really choice. Now all I do is give people the shits.

He finds LIZ's wedding ring where she left it on the table.

> FREDDIE (holding it up, talking at the door through which she's just exited) Can I give you a ring ?
> Ok, and I'll phone you later.

FREDDIE slips the ring on his little finger. Holds it up to look at it. Considers wearing it. Decides against it. Goes to slip it off but can't budge it.

> FREDDIE Shit !

Frantically he pulls at the thing. It's stuck. He goes to his kitchen area, looking for soap. Of course there is none.

> FREDDIE Soap !

Goes out

> FREDDIE. (calling out) Sheila ! *Sheila* ! Help!

A moment later the window slides open and GARETH climbs through, still clad in his Gorilla costume and still carrying his suitcase which we notice exactly resembles the one that LIZ has been carrying. He puts the one he's carrying down and goes over to the one LIZ has opened.

He checks to make sure that it's safe to do so and quickly opens a secret panel in the lid of his suitcase.

A small, furry looking animal drops out - lifeless. He shakes it, trying to coax it back into life with a stream of anxious Welsh. He puts the stethoscope on and checks for a heartbeat.

> GARETH. Don't tell me they've used too much chloroform again !

He shakes it again- violently.

> GARETH Come on, Jesus ! Wake up !

He bangs the animal's head on the table, then tries some mouth to mouth just as: the door opens, LIZ re-enters, takes one look at what appears to be a Gorilla about to devour a large rat and SCREAMS

GARETH drops the otter, grabs LIZ and puts a hand over her mouth.

>GARETH. Please don't scream.

She struggles against his hold.

>GARETH. Look, I can explain everything if you don't scream. Please!

She stops struggling. Cautiously, he releases his grip and closes the door behind them.

>LIZ. I'm not alone, I've got friends !

>GARETH (picking the otter up, stroking it)
>The poor little bugger's had a heart attack. I was just trying to give it some mouth to mouth.

>LIZ. A rat !

>GARETH. Actually- it's ... it's a rare Welsh otter.

LIZ notices the two suitcases.

>LIZ. My suitcase !

>GARETH. Yes, it appears there's been a mix up. You ah, haven't seen a snake have you ? There was a largish Zambesi python in there as well.

>LIZ. What !?

GARETH hunts around under the bed.

GARETH. They're the ones that like rats. Actually they'll eat anything: cats, a small dog, pet rabbits, hell of a thing to keep happy.

LIZ. Jesus !

GARETH (gives up looking for the snake) I dunno- at least it's alive I suppose. That's something.

LIZ. (slow dawning realisation) You- you've smuggled that animal in my suitcase.

GARETH. My suitcase.

LIZ. Which I carried through customs.

GARETH. Oh there's no risk, it's not like drugs or anything. Well - I admit the sniffer dogs are a worry, but they're not into otter or snake really, (trying to make light of it) they only go for the hardstuff. .

LIZ. I could've been arrested.

GARETH. Look - it wasn't your bag.

LIZ. I carried it. You can go to gaol for this sort of thing.

GARETH. Oh aye, but you didn't know what was inside.

LIZ. So ?

GARETH. So - no sweat - literally. I mean you're cool. They can sense that. They look at your pupils, to see whether they're enlarged or not. What you don't know doesn't hurt you. Me ? I was shaking like a leaf. And of course they searched my bag - sorry your bag - with a fine tooth comb.

She goes straight to check her suitcase.

LIZ. I just hope my photographs are here.

GARETH. It was pretty embarrassing actually. I had to pretend to be gay. I said I was glad they were searching through it since I'd lost ten pounds in there somewhere and I was hoping they'd find it 'cause I needed it for the cab from the airport. They thought I was trying to bribe them - could've been really awkward. (chuckles a little self consciously)

LIZ. You think this is funny ? I could be in gaol.

GARETH. I doubt if they'd pick on an expectant mother.

LIZ. (angry) That's not the point. The point is you *used me*.

GARETH. No ! No that's not true. It was a mistake, it was a genuine mistake. You must've picked my bag up first.

LIZ hasn't got any easy answer to that.

GARETH. Did you check the label ?

She can't say she did.

GARETH. It's just unfortunate. We seem to have the same taste in suitcases.

LIZ. I'm not convinced.

GARETH. Well, you've got me over a barrel, that's for sure.

She regards him cooly.

GARETH. You could turn me in.

LIZ. (folding her arms) You're lucky the photos are still there.

He smiles, relieved.

GARETH. They're great shots.

She somewhat aggressively turns back to re-ordering her suitcase.

LIZ. I see you've made a right mess of it !

GARETH. You can tell a lot about a person from what they travel with.

He picks up the otter and turns to his own case.

GARETH. I reckon you're probably about as poor as I am. Actually, it reminded me of going through my father's stuff just after he died. It does seem kind of rude prying into everything, holding his clothes, finding out little secrets, crying over the memory of something, his moth eaten rugby cap - or something as stupid as a toothbrush. (holding his own toothbrush, throwing it back in the case) So I thought well, I've lost both my parents now, I've got no profession left, might as well try the migrant thing, start from scratch.

LIZ. (scoffs) Profession !? Smuggling ?

GARETH. (with some dignity) I was a doctor.

LIZ. (faintly incredulous) You ! A doctor ?

GARETH (nods) That's how I heard about this private zoo in Adelaide. It's run by a sort of eccentric oncologist who I met once at a conference in London.

LIZ. Yeah, Adelaide can be like that.

GARETH. (shaking his head over the now dead otter) I'll get a fraction of the price for them stuffed.

LIZ. I think you're a con artist.

GARETH What ?

LIZ. Well, I mean look at this stuff (coming over to his bag) The priest's collar, the captain's hat, the stethoscope and white coat. They're costumes !

GARETH. Ok, so I'm a con artist. Have I done anything wrong ? I haven't hurt anybody. Well - the otter is unfortunate, but it could've been OK. They have a hell of a better life in Adelaide than the cold Welsh mountains waiting for some aristocrat's bullet or poacher's trap.

LIZ. You should be put in gaol.

GARETH. God I'm only trying to make a a few sovs. What else is a defrocked doctor supposed to do ?

LIZ. You're not a doctor.

GARETH. Not any more, true. But I was. 'Till about 5 years ago.

She regards him cynically.

GARETH. I was deregistered.

LIZ. I'm not surprised.

GARETH. I was one of the few people - well the only person really in the whole of North Wales who'd do home births. It was a threat to the Hospital system, you see. The establishment didn't like that, didn't trust it. Naturally I had to be made an example of.

LIZ. Naturally.

GARETH. So here I am - broke and qualified for nothing on the other side of the world. I thought, if I'm going to go on the dole might as well be in a warm country - preferably one that speaks a good broken English. (indicating the suitcase) This little enterprise was supposed to be my grub stake.

He sighs closes his case puts it on the ground. She also finishes with her repacking and puts her case down.

GARETH. What about yourself?

LIZ. I trained as a nurse. In Brisbane.

GARETH. No kidding, really ? You're having me on.

LIZ. Couldn't you tell from the uniform ?

GARETH. Look, I'm really sorry about this whole thing.

LIZ Yeah.

He goes over to FREDDIE's "kitchen" area.

GARETH. Glass of water or …

LIZ. I'm fine thanks.

She goes and sits down. On one of the milk crates. There's a slight pause, he drinks. Neither of them has anywhere else to go really.

GARETH. You - ah waiting for someone ?

LIZ. No. You ?

GARETH Oh, no.

Another pause.

GARETH. Been travelling long ?

LIZ. Long enough.

GARETH. I've never been outside the UK before. Bit of a white-knuckle flyer. Don't like being that far off the ground. Seems highly unnatural to me. Took a hell of a lot of Irish whisky to get me to Heathrow I'll tell you that.

Another pause.

GARETH Well …

He comes over picks up his suitcase.

She gets up, picks up hers.

They face each other.

But by now they've moved around so much that again neither is sure which case is which. Momentary confusion. She puts hers down again.

>GARETH. Oh … ahm … sorry…

They swap cases.

>GARETH. Hell of a thing.

They look at the case the other person's got, decide it was right the first time, swap cases back.

This time LIZ checks hers by opening it briefly. Wrong again.

So they swap back again. Stand there facing each other for a moment.

>GARETH. What the hell - I find you very attractive.

>LIZ. (rolling her eyes) Hoh !

>GARETH. You know something - you remind me of Sophie Loren.

>LIZ. No.

>GARETH You do.

>LIZ. I don't look anything like her.

>GARETH. You've got those same dark, zany good looks. Brown skin and all…

>LIZ. Stop it.

>GARETH. It's funny.

>LIZ What ?

GARETH. I was just thinking you're the sort of girl my mother would've liked me to settle down with. She always said, "Elwyn, find a nurse, son. They're reliable. They won't let you down."

She laughs, he smiles with her.

GARETH. I think that's the only reason she wanted me to be a doctor.

Again a pause.

GARETH. You know that's great when you laugh. They say laughter is the first sign of sexual attraction.

LIZ stops smiling.

GARETH laughs and she can't help herself, she laughs with him.

GARETH. You know you've got the sort of eyes a bloke could fall into ...

THE HAPPY HOUR MUSIC can be heard starting up outside

GARETH takes a step towards her, they seem on the point of embracing, LIZ doesn't resist. Slowly, inexorably he takes her in his arms and together they waltz out the door in the direction of the party.

GARETH. Sorry about the costume.

LIZ. Oh- I like a hairy man.

GARETH. I think yours is great.

LIZ. What ?

GARETH. Your costume.

LIZ. What costume ?

GARETH. That whole single mother idea, it's very now, it's witty I like it.

LIZ It's not a costume!!

GARETH stops dancing out in the Hallway. LIZ closes the door. They're gone.

HAPPY HOUR

Shortly after witnessing the previous three scenes everyone moves towards the source of the "HAPPY HOUR" MUSIC out the back: a largish TV/Dining room which has been cleared and decorated with balloons and streamers for a party.

Up one end of the room is a small stage where SHEILA and ROSIE provide 60/40 dance music (violin, casiotone, maracas and drum machine). Above "the band" is a horseshoe shaped banner announcing "*Linga Longer* Happy Hour."

At the extreme other end of the room (where people come in), MORREY is selling "broken pies", raffle tickets, punch and warm pikelets which he heats up by pressing down on them with an old electric iron.

On the floor, in a cleared space in the middle, GARETH and LIZ are still arm in arm, dancing.

> MORREY. (at a table near the door) Pikelets, nice warm pikelets. Broken pies half price. Get your punch and raffle tickets here, ladies and gentlemen, We're raffling off a lovely smoked chicken here tonight. (indicating a large, covered silver server beside him - which presumably contains the bird)

Where possible people are encouraged to dance, involving them for a little while in a kind of old-style, dance and singalong around the piano type situation. It's the music and communality of a pre-television era.

Eventually, the song/dance number comes to an end. SHIELA turns to the microphone on stage.

> SHEILA. Welcome, welcome ladies and gentlemen to the *Linga Longa* Happy Hour, a little monthly get together which all of us here at No. 26 like to share with our very dearest friends. As you know this is a group participation thing where everyone's got to do a number so who'd like to go first and be a star for 5 minutues ?

Nervously FREDDIE puts his hand up.

> SHEILA. Oh thank you Freddie, that's the spirit, let's break the
> ice with a true professional.

DRUM ROLL

> SHEILA. Ladies and Gentlemen, direct from a sell-out season at the Mildura Arts Festival, the funniest man never to have been to Edinburgh,

BIG DRUM ROLL - CLIMAX

> SHEILA. Mr. Freddie Feelgood !

Moderate applause as FREDDIE clasps his hands above his head and threads his way through the crowd towards the stage.

As he passes GARETH (still in his gorilla costume - LIZ in her Arabian outfit):

> GARETH. (peeved) I thought you said this was supposed to be a costume party.

Clearly nobody else except a mere handful, have got costumes on. FREDDIE just smiles weakly back at him and makes his almost trance-like progress towards the stage. As the takes the microphone we notice that SHEILA, as well as the name change, has obviously encouraged FREDDIE to discard his black clothes in favour of an incredibly kitcsh calypso outfit (bright Hawaiian shirt etc.). To cap it off he's even wearing a clown's red nose.

FREDDIE is really sweating, terrified of the ordeal before him. He shuffles through his prompt cards, there's a real hiatus. He taps the microphone, blows into it.

>FREDDIE. (nervous) It's really funny, you know, my mother, god rest her soul, always said to me- FREDDIE, be alert, son. (pause two, three) The world needs lerts.

DEAD SILENCE. Not a sound. Not even a snigger.

He bites his lip, his hands shaking like a drummers as he desperately hunts through his cards. Looking for a better joke.

>FREDDIE. Ah- my father on the other hand, well he might've been a slow learner but he had a heart of gold. He, he did things for me. He, he, took me to school. (pause two three) He had to, we were in the same class.

ROSIE does a sort of "BA BOOM" accompaniment on the DRUMS.

But apart from that - again DEAD SILENCE. Nothing. You can hear a pin drop.
FREDDIE is on the verge of tears.

>FREDDIE. I can't do this SheilA. I told you it was no good.
>
>SHEILA. (like talking to a dog) Freddie ! *Stay* !

Gulping, shaking FREDDIE turns back to the ordeal of the microphone. He searches to decipher another card through his violent shaking.

>MORREY. (down the back) I preferred his black period.

Some LAUGHTER at that. But it completely throws FREDDIE his cards fly everywhere.

> FREDDIE. Oh !

He gets on his hands and knees to retrieve them.

> SHEILA. Forgodsake, Freddie, *improvise* !
>
> FREDDIE. It's no good, Sheila, I can't do it.
>
> SHEILA. You'll do it now or you'll never work again.
>
> MORREY. Get him off. (slow hand clapping). Off!

FREDDIE clears his throat, tries again - without cards.

> FREDDIE. Funny thing happened to me on the way to the show tonight, ladies and gentlemen. (pause)
>
> MORREY. That's good, cause nothing funny's happened since you arrived.

BIG RESPONSE, MORREY nearly kills himself LAUGHING.

> FREDDIE. I got hit by a duck.

SHEILA LAUGHS uproariously, obviously forcing it, encouraging ROSIE to do the same.

FREDDIE glares at MORREY.

> FREDDIE. As I sat there on the roadside bleeding (indicates his arm, still in a sling) I said to the duck what's that snail doing over

there on the highway ? The duck said- "Oh about half a mile an hour".

SHEILA and ROSIE really kill themselves laughing.

MORREY. Get him off. Get him off !

FREDDIE. Morrey, do you know masturbation (softly) makes you deaf ?

MORREY Pardon ?

NOT A BAD LAUGH from that. It gives FREDDIE some of his courage back.

FREDDIE. Anyway, the duck said to me, look I'm sorry about this but you know it's a proven statistical fact that most accidents occur within 5 kilometers of where you live ? Oh, I said, is that why everyone's trying to leave home ?

Riotous LAUGHTER from SHEILA and ROSIE. FREDDIE throws the rest of his cards away.

>FREDDIE. "God" he said, looking at my arm, "I hope you don't bleed to death. I said "so do I - I might end up getting buried in the wrong hole."
>
>MORREY. That'd be a grave mistake.
>
>FREDDIE. (calling for help) *Sheila*!
>
>SHEILA. Stop it Morrey, leave the boy alone.
>
>FREDDIE. This is Morrey Price, ladies and gentlemen. As you can see from the delicate cuisine on sale tonight he's the cook around here - with the sort of face that shipped a thousand lunches.

SHIELA and ROSIE LAUGH.

>FREDDIE. Morrey's a bit shakey these days so sometimes, if he's serving you, you get soup in your fly.
>
>MORREY. Bring on the tap dancers !
>
>FREDDIE. I'm sorry Morrey, I can't do tap dancing. I keep falling into the sink.

The LAUGHTER grows, fuelling FREDDIE's confidence.

>FREDDIE. Actually, Morrey's also the caretaker here, ladies and gentlemen. He keeps claiming he never puts the rent up faster than inflation - in Argentina.
>
>MORREY. Terrible. Get him off.

In the background SHEILA nods to ROSIE and ROSIE goes out.

> FREDDIE. As you can see from his miser's stoop, Morrey's probably going to end up a hunchback. I think that's why he just bought a wok - so he can iron his shirts.

Big RESPONSE from the audience.

> FREDDIE. And as I always say on a closing note, ladies and gentlemen - only the meek shall inherit the earth – er ... if that's Ok with the rest of you ...

Big MUSICAL WIND-UP.

> SHEILA. Ladies and Gentlemen, Mr. Freddie Feelgood !

FREDDIE blows kisses to the audience, his confidence returned, happy with the response.

As the APPLAUSE DIES.

> SHEILA. Don't slip away yet, Freddie, there's a little song I think you might be interested in. Yes, ladies and gentlemen this song is dedicated to a young man who didn't ask a lot of the world and gave back to it every bit as much as it gave him. A kindly bloke who always welcomes you with a smile in his heart.

The lights dim and ROSIE re-enters with a birthday cake glowing with candles. ROSIE and SHEILA lead the singing.

> EVERYBODY. (singing) Happy birthday to you. Happy birthday to you. Happy birthday dear Fred-die, happy birthday to you.

FREDDIE is overwhelmed.

ROSIE. Make a wish.

FREDDIE. This, this … is the happiest day of my life.

In tears and barely able to speak FREDDIE blows the candles out.

Just as the lights abruptly come on and we discover a haggard and desperate looking NICK standing by the switch, supporting himself with one arm leaning against the wall. His tie's askew, his suit's a mess - like he's just woken up in the gutter – which he literally has – where ROSIE dumped him. He holds a gun menacing them all.

NICK. Right, you bastards, *get out* ! All of you ! Out of my boarding house and don't ever darken it's doors again !

FREDDIE. 'Scuse me, mate, you're interrupting our Happy Hour.

NICK. The *last* Happy Hour I'm pleased to say.

GENERAL CONSTERNATION. His voice seems strangely slurred. He yawns, helps himself to a large tumbler of punch, immediately spits it out.

NICK. Cockroach piss !

MORREY. (proudly) There are no cockroaches here.

NICK. No, the rats have eaten them all.

ROSIE. That's a bit uncalled for, mate.

NICK. This brothel is *closed* !

SHEILA. Language, please !

NICK. (holding up a tiny cassette tape) I've got a conversation here with a known prostitute which I secretly recorded tonight in one of these very rooms. This woman subsequently *drugged* me and left me lying in the *gutter*.

ROSIE. Where you belong !

NICK. God only knows what debauchery she committed upon my person in the meantime. I shudder to think. I've suffered nothing but pain and humiliation and I've got bruises to prove it.

MORREY. Now, just a minute, fella. You're sailing pretty close to slander there. I run a respectable private hotel .

NICK. "*Ran*" I think is the operative word.

MORREY. What ?

NICK. You're fired, derro.

MORREY. Well, actually sir, I quite agree with you it's in terrible shape. I've warned them, I've told them they've got to keep their doors open. I run a tight ship here, I've worked my fingers to the bone.

NICK. *Shuddup*! (producing it from his coat) This contract of sale gives my holding company title to the property as of 5 o'clock this afternoon. In the general interests of community health I'm now ordering you to vacate the premises immediately.

SHEILA. You can't throw us out. We - we belong here. Some of us have lived here for years. (breaking down) This is our *home*.

FREDDIE. I'm a protected tenant. We all are.

MURMURS of ASSENT from the crowd.

NICK. Not if the place is condemned.

FREDDIE. Well, we'll just have to squat it out. Possession's nine tenths of the law isn't it? You've got a fight on your hands Pal. We've got friends in low places.

SHEILA. I'm too old for that Freddie.

FREDDIE. We have to fight it Sheila. We can't let them walk over us. (to NICK) We're not moving!

MORREY. Here, here!

NICK. I've just phoned the Chapel Street police station and I'm happy to announce that they're on their way. I suggest that unless all of you wish to spend the night in gaol on vice and drug charges you should pack your squalid belongings and leave the dump immediately.

SHEILA. He's bluffing, surely. Where else are we going to go this time of night.

ROSIE. We're not moving.

FREDDIE. That's right.

MORREY. The cops can't arrest all of us.

FREDDIE. Yeah, so stick it up your arse you yuppie bastard.

NICK. If you don't go, dog's breath, this dump might just have a sudden accident with a lighted match and a drum of kerosene. And as far as I'm concerned it's good riddance to bad rubbish.

LIZ. (from down the back) Does that include me, Nick ?

NICK blinks, shakes his head. LIZ comes forward.

NICK. (stunned) Liz !

LIZ. Long time no see.

ROSIE. (equally shocked) This is Nick ? *Your* Nick ?

NICK. (focused only on LIZ) What are you doing here - this place, it's the pits.

LIZ. I'm staying here.

NICK. How can you have fallen so low !

Then he notices it for the first time.

NICK. My god ! You're pregnant ! In a brothel !

GARETH. (stepping in) Hey, listen, pal, you're pretty free with your tongue.

FREDDIE manages to head off GARETH, calming him down.

NICK. I came here half intending to commit suicide I was so depressed about losing you. You left me without so much as one word in, in… (tries to calculate)

Finally, ROSIE steps in.

> ROSIE. Yes - how long was it, Nick?
>
> NICK. I dunno, a long time. Months.
>
> ROSIE. Eight months ?
>
> NICK. Eight months, 19 days 12 hours and 37 minutes.
>
> MORREY. Congratulations, Dad.

NICK takes LIZ by the hand

> NICK. Let me get you out of here.
>
> GARETH. Just a second, mate !

GARETH grabs her other hand.

> GARETH. Liz is staying with me.
>
> ROSIE. This is ridiculous, I brought her here, she's staying in my room.
>
> MORREY. Hang on, this place is full, there are no vacancies.
>
> SHEILA. There's a room upstairs.
>
> MORREY. It's taken.
>
> NICK. Nobody's staying anywhere, the place is condemned.
>
> GARETH. (including LIZ) We'll go somewhere else then.

FREDDIE. You can't stay here mate, you're a foreigner.

LIZ. Not if I marry him.

NICK. (despairing) *Liz*!

GARETH. Perfect. Just the three of us. Somewhere quiet.

LIZ. I said marriage, I didn't say we'd live together.

GARETH. Eh ?

LIZ. I'm putting the child up for adoption.

ROSIE. No, Lizzie !

LIZ. I *have* to. I mean look at me, I can't make that sort of commitment.

GARETH. You can if I'm with you.

ROSIE. *I'm* supporting LIZ, do you mind, we're going to look after this baby ourselves. It's all been worked out.

SHEILA. That settles it, you and the baby are both staying here. We'll all look after you. This is what we always wanted, isn't it, Rosie ? A real family at last.

SHEILA puts another arm around LIZ.

NICK. Forgodsake ! It's *my* baby !

ROSIE. Maybe.

NICK. I know it's mine.

LIZ. I wouldn't count on it.

NICK. What ?

FREDDIE. This is fantastic, it's like Jesus, Mary and Joseph. We must be in Bethlehem.

MORREY. No one's staying in any more rooms. This House is *full* ! And that's final. There are no vacancies.

FREDDIE. What are you talking about? This nerd's going to pull the place down.

ROSIE. No he's not.

NICK. Oh yes I am.

ROSIE. I don't think you'll be turning the *Linga Longa*
into a wedding reception centre, Nick, not once
the Licensing Squad get a glimpse of this …
Show him Morrey.

MORREY. What ?

ROSIE. The photos.

MORREY. Oh yeah.

MORREY digs into his coat pocket and produces a polaroid. NICK takes it.

NICK. What ? A photo of someone's carpet ?

ROSIE snatches it off him.

ROSIE. Morrey ! You idiot. You've missed
him completely.

NICK LAUGHS derisively.

MORREY. You see sir, I did have your
interests at heart I hope you take this into
account.

SHEILA. *Morrey* ! You traitor !

NICK laughs even louder. The others look puzzled. ROSIE rummages in MORREY's pockets for another snap.

MORREY. Hey, who's that ? What's going on !

Frantically ROSIE rejects a couple more photos before hitting the jackpot.

ROSIE. (shoving it at NICK) There, that
should give you something to laugh about.

NICK's LAUGHTER stops, his eyes pop at the snap of him with the doll and the whip.

>NICK. This - this is a set up.

LIZ snatches the photo back off him.

>LIZ. Oh Nick !

It gets passed around. Now it's the others turn to LAUGH.

>NICK. I was drugged I tell you.

>FREDDIE. Rosie, beneath that rough exterior beats a harlot of gold.

>LIZ. How could you, Nick. How could you sink so low.

>NICK. It's a lie. She - she did it to me. (feeling for it) Where. . . where's my wallet?

>ROSIE. Where's these people's future ?

>NICK. … (I) feel so tired. (yawns) What have you done to me ?

>LIZ. What have you done to yourself, Nick ? What have you done to everyone who comes in contact with you? You're so absorbed with your quest for money that you can't even see beyond your own self interest. You've become cold and heartless. Effectively dead.

>NICK. Oh that's choice coming from someone who hitches herself to the first itinerant freeloader who stumbles by.

>LIZ. Oh - you'll end up with a big pile of cash no doubt. But you'll have lost the only thing

worth striving for: a bit of love and friendship, people's respect, the knowledge that money isn't everything.

NICK. You can talk ! Up the duff in brothel. That's really some achievement

LIZ. I left because you didn't want to have a child. At first I felt bad about that. I felt dishonest. Now - I couldn't care less.

NICK. This place is so full of deception I wonder if you're even really pregnant. You've probably stuffed a pillow up your jumper to get the sympathy vote.

GARETH. Right, that's it.

GARETH moves in on NICK, NICK goes to tear LIZ's shirt off to reveal the "pillow". In the melee that follows SHEILA and ROSIE try to stop NICK, FREDDIE tries to stop GARETH and beneath it all is LIZ - who lets out a terrific SCREAM.

Every one stops.

MORREY. Could I interest any one in a raffle ticket ?

LIZ. It's coming.

Now a different sort of panic sets in. As LIZ goes into labour:

ROSIE. Morrey call an ambulance.

GARETH. help me carry her ...

FREDDIE. Here let me ...

NICK. Do you mind, she's virtually my wife. I'm the father of her child.

GARETH. Yes but I'm going to marry her.

MORREY. What's the number ?

SHEILA. Forget the ambulance call a cab.

SHEILA, ROSIE, FREDDIE, GARETH, and NICK lift LIZ above their heads and carry her out the door heading for hospital, still arguing and LIZ panting. This effectively leaves MORREY alone with the crowd.

MORREY. Wait ! Wait ! I'm coming too…

But his tenants, the new landlord and the blow-ins have all gone.

MORREY. That's right, that's right, don't worry about me. I'll be fine. I'll see everyone out, clean up the mess, cash in the bottles - as usual. Oh yes, don't you worry about that. Go on, go off to the hospital while I hold the fort as *I usually do* from my commodious 8 by 12 foot room - where nobody comes to visit me. Call that a room, more like a large WC. And talk about a view ! Another brick wall - that's my view, not that I can see it.

Miffed, he works his way back to the stage where the large silver server waits. He takes off his hat and dumps in the raffle tickets he's managed to sell tonight.

MORREY. (launching straight into it) Alright the winner of the raffle is (peremptorily pulling a ticket out) Green ticket number 54 (adjust) Would the owner of Green 54 come and get their chook.

As the LUCKY WINNER comes up on stage MORREY opens the lid of the silver server to reveal:

The huge ferocious gaping mouth of GARETH's missing python which looks like it's just eaten the smoked chicken prize.

MORREY looks at the audience. Senses their reaction. Turns to face the python. Reacts. Closes the lid.

PANIC breaks out and so do the lights.

BLACKOUT

Sound of the SILVER SERVER DROPPING. People running for the nearest available exit.

END MUSIC

Linden Art Centre 1989

CRITICAL RECEPTION

THE AGE

Wednesday 5 April 1989

Comic slices of St Kilda life from TheatreWorks

THIS is the second occasion on which playwright Paul Davies has used the once-gracious St Kilda mansion 'Linden' in Acland Street to stage one of his inventive location dramas.

On the first occasion, in 'Living Rooms', the audience was taken on a peripatetic journey around the house. In each of the three main rooms — the parlor, the gallery and a scruffy back room — an episode in the house's history was enacted. The audience itself was split into three groups which meant that most of them saw the three episodes, set in 1901, 1972 and the present day, in non-chronological order.

In 'Full House — No Vacancies' the approach is similar, except that the three episodes occur in the same time frame, and mesh more closely into one another. So in that sense it doesn't matter where you start your theatrical journey. Sooner or later you will wind up encountering the three residents of the rundown Lings Longa boarding house — Sheila, Rosie and Freddie — and their unwelcome guests.

Sheila, a grand actress of European

REVIEW

Theatre

LEONARD RADIC

Full House — No Vacancies by Paul Davies (TheatreWorks, at 26 Acland Street, St Kilda).

extraction and dubious talent, lives in costumed splendor in the large front room waiting as always for the phone to ring. Rosie, a therapeutic masseuse — at least that's her story and she's sticking to it — lives across the hallway, dispensing warmth and relaxation, while Freddie, a radical cabaret artiste and unfunny funnyman, lives with his milk crates, Ravel and rack of funny noses in the squalid room at the back.

At various times in the evening their lives are invaded by Gareth, a Welsh freedom fighter in gorilla suit; Liz, a heavily pregnant backpacker newly returned from overseas; Morrey, the crazy gun-toting caretaker; and Nick, a sinister figure in the real estate business

who plans to raze the Linga Longa and erect a carpark in its place.

As usual, Davies draws his characters with broad brush strokes. The writing is rather flat in places, while the jigsaw pieces of the plot never quite fit together. None the less, the piece is held together by the sheer energy of the players who leap in and out of doors, windows and cupboards in the best French farce tradition.

The production, by Robin Laurie, is lively and entertaining. Somehow the running, jumping and standing still is synchronised so that the audience is never kept waiting. At the end everyone troops off to the communal dining room where the cast stage an impromptu concert designed to send the audience off home in a happy frame of mind.

This is not profound or daring theatre. But it is innovative, inventive, full of fun. As with 'Living Rooms', it also taps into the debate about property development in St Kilda. As a Comedy Festival event, it more than earns its keep.

IN**THEA**TRE

FULL HOUSE, NO VACANCIES

Theatreworks

As I walked up Ackland Street, making my way towards Linden, the venue for Full House, No Vacancies, I was anticipating an orthodox evening of theatre — one stage, one set of seats for the audience, and very few props. I also assumed that I was to be a passive viewer, watching from the anonymity of a darkened theatre. I could not have been more mistaken.

Number 26, Ackland Street turned out to be the Linga Longa Private Boarding House, and the audience were the guests of its residents at a lively and surprising happy hour, complete with chook raffle. After being greeted at reception, I was invited to adjourn to Sheila's room, but not until given the signal to do so. Having arrived early, this gave me the opportunity to read the notices, typical of a run-down St.Kilda boarding house. "Definitely no back packers" — that didn't include me — "No cooking in the rooms" — thankfully I had already had dinner — "No guests in the rooms or you will be thrown out!" — rather strict rule!

I walked up to the door of Sheila's (Valentina Levawicz) room, a shabby and faded material rose hanging next to her name, which was written with lavish swirls and curls. I caught myself wondering what kind of woman Sheila could be. The next moment I found out, for the

Caroline Howards and Roger Sellock in Theatrework's Full House, No Vacancies

woman herself appeared in the crowded and busy hallway, dressed in silky pants with a matching top, curlers in hair and feather slippers on feet. She introduced herself, carrying a bowl of punch and speaking with a Russian accent. The next moment a broom was shoved between my feet as a middle-aged caretaker scrounged for dust and cigarette butts. A phone rang, a call for Freddy Finally, a self-pitying, gloom-struck, unsuccessful stand-up comic. Next Liz arrived at the door, wearing a tent dress in an effort to conceal what was blatantly obvious. Then Rosie, a professional "relaxation" therapist, appeared standing next to me, waving to Liz, checking out the guests and bopping to the Beatles music playing in the background. It was difficult trying to work out who was acting and who was not. Actually everyone was and we were just beginning to realise this fact.

Full House, No Vacancies is a brilliantly conceived story of one particular evening in a St Kilda boarding house. Each character is trying to keep a grasp of their sanity and integrity while trying to avoid the commonplace occurrences of the 1980's. The Linga Longa is a sanctuary, free from Dial-A-Dinos, push button telephones, property developers and remote-control television. It's residents live from day to day, striving to maintain the institution of St.Kilda, whilst still holding on to the glory of their youthful ambitions.

My advice is to grab a tambourine, visit the residents of 26 Ackland Street, and join in at the Linga Longa sing-along. You might even win the chook.

★ Elizabeth Wortley

Theatreworks, the St Kilda-based company which largely pioneered this sort of "location theatre", contributes *Full House/No Vacancies*, an ingenious play by Paul Davies about characters living in a St Kilda boarding house. It is performed at Linden, a rehabilitated mansion which was a boarding house. The audience is divided into three rooms and there sees different versions of the same half-hour leading up to the final act. *the Linga Longa Hotel's Happy Hour*. It reminds me, in structure, of Alan Ayckbourn's *The Norman Conquests* except that everything happens simultaneously, demanding nice timing from the cast. It is performed with tremendous energy, with particularly entertaining performances from Brian Nankervis as the failed comic Freddie Finally and Carolyn Howard as the reformed prostitute Rosie.

Theatreworks lets loose on *Full House/No Vacancies* at Linden

ALISON CROGGON

MELBOURNE STAR OBSERVER

Comedy About St Kilda

Full House - No Vacancies
by Paul Davies
Theatreworks

In St Kilda in the 1920's, palatial mansions were internally carved up into private living spaces, apartments.

Paul Davies, author of Theatreworks' latest offering, carves up the lives of such tenants in the 1980's who are now living under the threat of eviction. Yuppies are taking over one of the last bastions of Melbourne bohemia: St Kilda.

Davies' work as writer and actor in *Stroming Mont Albert by Tram*, *Breaking Up In Balwyn* (on river boat The Yarra Queen) and *Living Rooms* (in an historic mansion), has written yet another hit which will "linga longa", unlike the private hotel Linga Longa he writes about.

Full House has many of the ingredients that make it a roaring comic contribution to the Comedy Festival. Let me explain.

The audience arrive at Linga Longa (Linden) to be greeted at the door with a neon sign plastered over the entrance announcing "Full House. No Vancancies". The owner, Morrey, who has no sight and less patience, snarls at the guests and points them in the direction of doormat which reads: "Wipe Ya Bloody Feet".

Morrey assumes that we have arrived for the Happy Hour, and so exchanges our invitations for tickets in the Linga Longa chook raffle. Is the picture emerging?

We, the guests, are then divided up into three groups and shoved into one of the three bedrooms where the action takes place. Sheilla, a nouveau nostalgia queen, is our first port of call. What a bedroom! So many frills and so much make-up!

Sheilla is face-packed and waiting for a call from her agent. It's to be her big break back into showbiz. Sadly, the only one to ring is a charity-bent priest in search of a church concert pianist. Sheilla has the most novel way of heating party pies: in her electric blanket.

The second bedroom belongs to Rosie, though it could belong to any number of you whose taste stopped in 1973. Rosie, a post modern tragedy and reformed prostitute in her 30's, was never told that palms, leopard-skin doonas and water beds are just so out of date. Nevertheless, she has turned to massage and possibly would treat her patients to a naturopathic hump if a scandal was in need of recording.

Freddie, finally, inhabits the last bedroom. For most of the play he's in everybody else's room. Freddie is a stand-up comic who has never seen the lights of Edinburgh, refuses to face a crowd and believes as a consequence that "people are bastards and the World's stuffed."

Who can dispute such a vivid analysis of his predicament? Surely not Liz, an ex-nurse and now pregnant back-packer who has come to stay; or Nick, the real estate agent (sleazebag) who is rumoured to have bought the building. Maybe Freddie may find such consolation in Gareth, a Welsh shearer who has turned to bird smuggling. But what hope does he really have - even the guests forget his birthday - or do they?

Eventually we all end up in the living room for a riotous happy hour with all the tennants and guests. I didn't win the chook raffle, but I did enjoy an innovative, physical comedy which celebrated the lives of St Kilda's locals. Theatreworks is assured of one thing: a full house with no vacancies!

A word of warning: Don't eat the party pies, and "Wipe Ya Bloody Feet"!

•Maurice Lawlor

REVIEWS

Linden itself on a previous occasion) and *Full House* is as good an example of the company's adventurous house-style as any. It is also typical of the generally lightweight content of TheatreWorks shows: they don't make many demands upon their audiences but they're usually great fun!

It is, in the end, heartening and pleasing to see some of the interesting work of the smaller companies getting into print; it has certainly deserved it.

GEOFFREY MILNE

Geoffrey Milne is principal tutor in drama at La Trobe University and drama critic for the *Melbourne Herald*.

House of fun in St Kilda

COMEDY

Full House, No Vacancies
By Paul Davies. Presented by Theatre-Works. Mon-Sat 8.30 pm, matinees Wednesday 1.30 pm and Saturday 5 pm at Linden, 26 Acland St, St Kilda, until April 22. Bookings 650-1977 or Bass
Reviewed by Carolyn O'Donnell

LIZ the pregnant backpacker has arrived, Morrey is shooting intruders and semi-talented comic, Freddie, has finally been beaten up by a bunch of bikies.

Meanwhile, the odd real estate developer and Welsh immigrant are hiding in wardrobes and jumping through windows.

It's just a typical night at the Linga Longa Hotel located, where else, in St Kilda. That is to say, old St Kilda.

In the tradition of *Living Rooms* (also by Paul Davies) comes *Full House, No Vacancies*, an ambulatory piece which takes the audience, literally, through the lives (and rooms) of people whose lives revolve around the Hotel.

Linden, a restored Victorian mansion, which alternates as an art gallery, is ideally suited to the play.

Described by TheatreWorks as "location theatre", the audience is split into three during the events leading up to the "happy hour" in rooms belonging to three very different characters.

Seeing what are essentially the same events from three different perspectives, the audience can piece together the sequence as a whole, while entertained by the idiosyncracies of the three residents involved.

The characters, all exaggerated to some extent, are vivid reflection of many of St Kilda's more interesting personas. *Full House, No Vacancies* is an example of traditional theatre meeting the distilled St Kilda Experience. It is a vibrant, lively production combining elements of comedy and drama.

The play suffers from some weak moments, especially some padding at times, and occasionally the script is a little flat and contrived.

However, the sheer energy of the piece carries the audience along and draws it into what is exceptionally well synchronised slice-of-life theatre. But among the froth and the trauma lies a strong anti-development message.

MELBOURNE TUESDAY APRIL 4, 1989

The Herald

Quintessentially St Kilda, *Full House, No Vacancies* makes a plea not only to preserve a unique bayside suburb, but places generally which because of their bohemian nature or mix of residents give a city character and stop it becoming just another bland collection of skyscrapers.

The design, by Pippa, is of note each detailed bedroom capturing the essence of its occupant utterly.

The communal diningroom, where the denouement (a mixture of surprise and twisted cliche) takes place, is appropriately dagsville.

For a theatre off the beaten floorboards, this is it. Generally *Full House, No Vacancies* is lots of fun and regular TheatreWorks patrons should not be disappointed, either.

The MELBOURNE REPORT

Fern Voller

I drove passed it the first time. There didn't seem to be anything on at Linden. The only building lit up was the Linga Longa Hotel with its illuminous sign 'Full House No Vacancies'. It was my destination.

Despite the outrageous comedy, Paul Davies latest play *Full House No Vacancies* (Apr 3-May 6)does have a serious theme. Once infamous for its drug addicts, prostitutes, street kids, drunks and generally seedy way of life, St Kilda is on the move. It has become trendy, home to the yuppies, the developers and the entourage which goes with real estate on the rise. Not all agree that the change is for the good. Indeed, St Kilda is suffering from an identity crisis.

We first meet Morrey (Phil Sumner) the caretaker. He suffers from agoraphobia, wears an eyepatch, grows drugs in the cellar and hates the guests. But his special hate is back packers. Morrey is 'the tragedy of the little man'. He also has a bit of a thing for Sheila. Originally from the USSR and a long term guest, Sheila (Valentina Levkowicz) is a faded star who now waits and hopes for guest spots on commercials. Underneath, all the perfume and other paraphernalia, she has a heart of gold and diseased liver. Enter Freddie Finally (Brian Nankervis), a slightly punk stand-up comic in the midst of a nervous breakdown on his thirtieth birthday.

This devotee of Lenny Bruce and The Smiths carries a torch for a reformed hooker, called Rosie (Carolyn Howard). Having cleaned up her act she is now into safe sex and stress management. She is also out to get Nick (Roger Selleck), the developer, who wants to turn the Linga Longa into a carpark. Rosie has a bit of a thing for an eight and a half months pregnant hippy called Liz (Laura LaHuada) who is the estranged love of Nick. The plot gets even more complicated when Liz falls for Gareth (Merlyn Owen), a back packer from the UK whom Freddie has smuggled into the hotel.

It is quite a remarkable feat that all the action takes place simulutaneously as the audience (which is divided into groups) moves from boudoir to boudoir. Indeed, it is a remarkable performance from the beginning to Freddie Finally's stand-up routine and Liz and Gareth's love song.

Directed by Robin Laurie and produced by Theatre works, *Full House No Vacancies* is a theatrical event!

PAUL DAVIES *has again created another 'season extended' success with his* FULL HOUSE NO VACANCIES.

EMERALD HILL TIMES
30-3-89

Raymond J needs a holiday – Brian told us so

By CLAIRE FITZPATRICK

Seated on the fence outside Linden gallery in St Kilda, Raymond J. Bartholomeuz – poet, civil engineer, hot air balloonist, eminent author and recording star in his own right – plays with the camera, drawing it in with expressions of sorrow.

He is obviously in agony, his quivering, contorted body expressing the deepest emotions of a poet in torment.

Later in a quiet cafe, a man strongly resembling the melancholic bard, is bubbling with enthusiasm about the theatre, comedy and the inspiration he gets from school children.

While the transformation is noticeable, it is not so surprising. For Raymond J. Bartholomeuz is only one side to his creator, Brian Nankervis.

Indeed, since creating the satirical poet some years ago, Nankervis has been working at developing his character along a variety of lines.

He has just come from rehearsing a new Theatreworks play - Full House, No Vacancies - for the Comedy Festival. Written by Paul Davies, the play is set in a St Kilda boarding house and tells the story of a group of eccentric characters.

"There's a great feeling among us," he says. "It's an interesting play and satirical response to all the street poets who had bombarded Nankervis with their tragic work which, says Nankervis, "was largely incomprehensible to anyone else but themselves."

Raymond's formal career, however, was launched at The Last Laught Theatre Restaurant in Collingwood, where Nankervis was working as a waiter. It was during a show called Let The Blood Run Free and what had begun as a bit of a joke developed extensively.

"Sundays consisted of church, Sunday School, World Of Sport and the Dandenongs, capped off with Disneyland and reheated scones", he recalls. Those recollections of middle class suburbia have somehow crept into Raymond J's poetry.

But what of Nankervis? While the infamous street poet was reaching a much wider audience on television's Hey Hey It's Saturday, Nankervis was trying his hand at other things.

Often in theatrical relationships there is a danger of the creation overwhelming the creator. Nankervis is uncertain about this: "I suppose there is a danger that if you become so well known as Raymond J, producers are reluctant to approach you. But then again, if you're convincing this should not matter."

Nankervis is keen to do some serious acting. He is currently working as an "assimilated patient" for a Lincoln Institute program in which actors are employed to play patients for students to observe and practice on.

Nankervis sees it as a good discipline, particularly for developing improvisation skills, and in researching a role.

"In a play, to make sense of the script, you have to be aware of every facet of your character. For the Lincoln characters I write long detailed character backgrounds," he says.

Meanwhile, Raymond J has just finished some weekend tours of Sydney, Canberra and Brisbane, with Melbourne band, This Is Serious Mum. Working with TISM has been an exciting experience for Raymond J, but Nankervis remains dubious about audience reception. "TISM audiences tend to be terribly passionate," he says. "At midnight at the Paddington Leagues Club, they don't really want to listen to spoken poetry."

Nankervis has plans for Raymond to extend his musical career. The album Crayfish Frenzy contains some solid blues numbers and there is talk of touring with a band.

Meanwhile Raymond J is gearing up for a late show during The Comedy Festival with former Dodgy Brother Geoff Brooks, Lynda Gibson and Judy Pascoe.

After that the lad from Templestowe will continue to write more poetry. "I don't know," ponders Nankervis, "I think Raymond should perhaps go back to Jamaica for some sabbatical."

One thing is certain: if Raymond J does return to his home country, his mentor won't be left with nothing to do. In the words of the great poet himself. "I do not wait for trains anymore/They have never waited for me."

● Full House, No Vacancies opens at The Linden Gallery, 26 Acland Street, St Kilda, on April 3. Raymond J Bartholomeuz is also appearing in a late show, "A Night With Mr and Mrs Rump and Raymond J Bartholomeuz," at The Carlton Courthouse on April 6, 7, 8, and 13, 14, 15.

Raymond J without the restraining influence of Brian Nankervis, outside Linden Gallery in Acland Street.

OFFICIAL JOURNAL OF THE COUNCIL OF THE CITY OF ST. KILDA

St. Kilda Today

APRIL 1989

What's on in Heritage Week

Full House – No Vacancies

From the beginning of April, *Linden* Gallery in Acland Street will be transformed into the Linga Longa Private Hotel for the latest piece of 'location theatre' by Theatreworks written by Paul Davies, who wrote the highly successful *Living Rooms* which was also performed in *Linden*, and *Storming St. Kilda By Tram*, last year's Comedy Festival hit which moved audiences - literally – for 11 weeks!

Fullhouse – No Vacancies is on for a limited season, Mondays to Saturdays 8.30pm, with matinees Wednesdays 1.30pm and Saturdays 5.00pm. Full price $19.99, concessions $15.99; Wednesday matinees: $10.99. Group booking enquiries 534 4879/534 8986. Bookings essential: BASS 11500 or 650 1977. Venue: "Linden", Acland Street, St. Kilda.

Full House, No Vacancies is a play about the changing face of St. Kilda, and the way it affects the residents at the Linga Longa boarding house.
The play's theme and setting are particularly appropriate for Heritage Week. It opens April 3 and continues through to the end of Heritage Week on Saturday 22. Further details Theatreworks phone 534 4879. Venue: *Linden*, 26 Acland Street, St. Kilda.

wednesday april 12, issue no 41, 1989

FULL HOUSE, NO VACANCIES

Theatreworks

As I walked up Ackland Street, making my way towards Linden, the venue for Full House, No Vacancies, I was anticipating an orthodox evening of theatre — one stage, one set of seats for the audience, and very few props. I also assumed that I was to be a passive viewer, watching from the anonymity of a darkened theatre. I could not have been more mistaken.

Number 26, Ackland Street turned out to be the Linga Longa Private Boarding House, and the audience were the guests of its residents at a lively and surprising happy hour, complete with cheap raffle. After being greeted at reception, I was invited to adjourn to Sheila's room, but not until given the signal to do so. Having arrived early, this gave me the opportunity to read the notices typical of a run-down St Kilda boarding house. "Definitely no back packers" — that didn't include me — "No cooking in the rooms" — thankfully I had already had dinner — "No guests in the rooms or you will be thrown out" — rather strict rule!

I walked up to the door of Sheila's (Valentina Levowicz) room, a shabby and faded material rose hanging next to her name, which was written with lavish swirls and curls. I caught myself wondering what kind of woman Sheila could be. The next moment I found out, for the woman herself appeared in the crowded and busy hallway, dressed in silly pants with a matching top, curlers in hair and feather slippers on feet. She introduced herself, carrying a bowl of punch and speaking with a Russian accent. The next moment a broom was shoved between my feet as a middle-aged caretaker scrimaged for dust and cigarette butts. A phone rang...a call for Freddy finally, a self-pitying, gloom struck, unsuccessful stand-up comic. Next Liz arrived at the door, wearing a tent dress in an effort to conceal what was blatantly obvious. Then Rosie, a professional 'relaxation' therapist, appeared standing next to me, waving to Liz, checking out the guests and bopping to the Beatles music playing in the background. It was difficult trying to work out who was acting and who was not. Actually everyone was and we were just beginning to realise this fact.

Full House, No Vacancies is a brilliantly conceived story of one particular evening in a St Kilda boarding house. Each character is trying to keep a grasp of their sanity and integrity while trying to avoid the commonplace occurrences of the 1980's. The Linga Longa is a sanctuary, free from Dial-A-Dinos, push button telephones, property developers and remote-control television. It's residents live from day to day, striving to maintain the institution of St Kilda, whilst still holding on to the glory of their youthful ambitions.

My advice is to grab a tambourine, visit the residents of 26 Ackland Street, and join in at the Linga Longa sing-along. You might even win the chook.

★ Elizabeth Wortley

Caroline Howards and Roger Selleck in Theatrework's Full House, No Vacancies

FULL HOUSE NO VACANCIES
LINDEN GALLERY

FULL HOUSE/NO VACANCIES is the latest comedy from Paul Davies and THEATREWORKS. Davies was the writer of the hugely popular *Storming St. Kilda By Tram* and he continues his string of "Location Theatre" hits with this delightful piece set in "Linden" — a former private hotel.

You enter the foyer of the Linga Longa Private Hotel after passing such endearing signs as "Tresspassers will be shot" and "Full House No Vacancies" and find your fellow punters standing around looking silly as they try and not notice such signs as 'No Backpackers' and a rather odd character on the red phone. Into this chaos arrives a very pregnant woman (with backpack) who is chased out by this aggressive little man. It is then explained that the happy hour is slightly delayed and could we please wait in the residents rooms.

The audience, having been split into three groups troop off to either Rosie's, Shelia's or Freddie's room and the fun begins. The story unfolds in each of the rooms and eventually you discover that Linga Longa is the sight of a redevelopment proposal. Freddie is a failed comic and his rescuer from his last performance Gareth is a Welsh nationalist, Shelia is waiting for a call from her agent and Rosie is a practitioner of relaxation massage, friend of Liz and her client is the redeveloper.

The splitting of the audience and the punctuation of the plot by out of sight devices like clocks chiming, gunshots, screams etc., creates an original and higly entertaining bedroom farce. Directed by Robin Laurie, the cast play it at the pace that farce demands — fast. The audience becomes immediately involved and intrigued by the plot and quite forgets the Happy Hour that awaits.

It is a mark of the quality of Paul Davies' writing that a Welsh nationalist, dressed in a gorilla suit, climbing through a St. Kilda boarding house window is internally logical to the play. It is also incredibly funny — normally if I see a gorilla suit I pick up my bag and leave.

The Happy Hour as a finale to a show is a theatrical cliche that usually means the author ran out of original ideas acts ago and is desperate for some way out of the mess — in *Full House / No Vacancies* it is the icing on the cake. A great night out.

J.H.

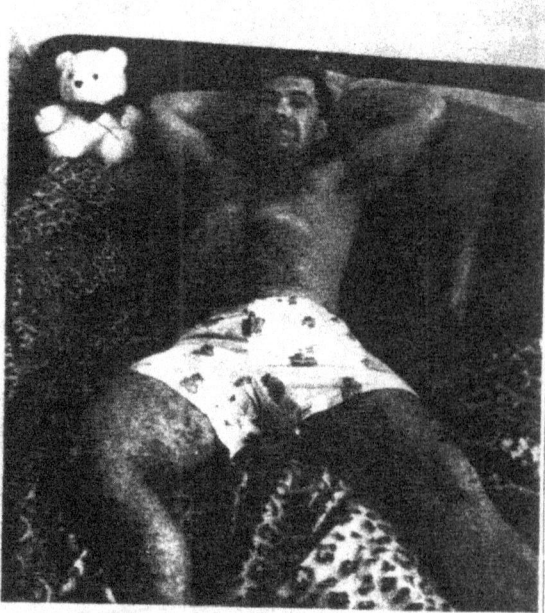

THE AGE, Saturday 15 April 1989

COMEDY FESTIVAL
Success launches humor as a serious business

THE third Melbourne Comedy Festival, which concludes tonight with the Troppo Carnivale at Luna Park, has advanced the cause of those seeking to create an event of international standing.

As Melbourne's annual comedy festival draws to an end, MARTIN FLANAGAN reflects on two weeks of laughter and tears.

The inaugural festival in 1987 created the sense that something new and unexpected was happening in the Garden State, but the second festival nearly disappeared down a hole not of its own making.

With the late withdrawal of the guest-of-honor, Monty Python's Graham Chapman, Phyllis Diller was cast in a role for which her long years in showbiz mainstream and many facelifts had not equipped her. She struggled on gamely, even managing to laugh during the news conference at which comic Bing Hitler appeared naked, but for the most part it was like watching Barbara Cartland read to an audience of beat poets.

This year the big top went up and stayed up, largely thanks to Mort Sahl (and, by extension, entrepreneur Simon Palomares who shouldered the financial risk of bringing him to Australia). The festival was like a stew with a laudable range of ingredients — the Sally Swain exhibition 'Great Housewives in Art' had not previously been seen outside New York or London — but it was Sahl who gave it body.

Here was an entertainer who addressed the intelligence of his audiences directly, which is probably why he created so much confusion. At the festival's introductory news conference, Sahl remarked that when he started his career he was told he was a radical, but now he was being called a moralist. Dave Allen leaned over to him and muttered in his ear, "Aren't they the same thing?"

If supposedly serious matters are often humorous, Mort Sahl reminded us that humor can also be deadly serious. His contribution to 'Humorists Read Humorists' was to read from the findings of the Warren Commission, the official inquiry into the assassination of his friend, US President John Kennedy. People laughed, which is precisely Sahl's point.

This year's festival had what Arthur Daley might call "muscle". It bucked and jumped and threw a few of its riders. Last year's 'Lawyers, Guns and Money' show, which employed local identities and not actors, did not quite make it as a farce and struck only glancing social blows. This year John Clarke joined the writing team and the resulting product, the 'Royale Commission', got down in earnest to the business of satire.

The point was that somewhere within the outrageous and wildly defamatory "revelations", there was usually an element of truth. When, for example, the actor cruelly misrepresenting Ross Oakley, the VFL commissioner, was forced to admit that netball, not football, was Victoria's most popular participation sport, there were some in the audience — mostly women — who did not laugh. They cheered.

Similarly, the Paul Davies play 'Full House' took as its emotional spring the battle in St Kilda between residents and developers. One had a sense throughout this year's festival that the compost heap in which we live was being turned over.

This year's festival was an undoubted commercial success, with 11 of the shows extending their seasons, but one senses that the festival is at a threshold and the decisions made over the next 12 months may prove critical in determining its eventual stature and character.

Comedy is a perilous business, but a repeat of 1988 could see the festival become a sort of Melbourne follies. It should be remembered that one of the triumphs of this year's festival was 'Humorists Read Humorists', an event without commercial precedent. If the festival is to be a world event, it must have a life of its own based purely on a commitment to humor and humor in all its forms.

Comedians Mort Sahl (right) and Dave Allen at the press conference that launched the festival for 1989.

FULL HOUSE, NO VACANCIES
Written by Paul Davies.
Theatreworks
Linden Gallery,
26 Acland Street, St Kilda.
Review:
CLAIRE FITZPATRICK

WE arrived at the Linga Longa Boarding House in St Kilda only to be met by the sign "Full House, No Vacancies".

After some deliberation with the caretaker, Morrie, an objectionable little man, the group was divided into three and ushered into various rooms. We waited patiently in the room of frustrated stand-up comic, Freddie.

Such an introduction sets the scene for a riotous evening of laughter and innovative theatre. An array of eccentric characters, including a Welsh freedom fighter in a gorilla suit and a dodgy real estate agent, pop in and out of the rooms as the story unfolds, giving a taste of life in a St Kilda boarding house.

Written by Paul Davies, *Full House, No Vacancies* is a clever piece of theatre which induces total audience involvement. Scenes are played to the three groups as they move from room to room.

The story is simple, touching on the topical issues of development in St Kilda which threatens to engulf the Linga Longa. It is laced with limp moralism which reaches its climax in the final scene.

This takes the form of a Happy Hour, where all is revealed in a cabaret.

Overall it makes for great entertainment and an hilarious night out and gets people involved in the true spirit of theatre.

Showing how Full House/No Vacancies got its name.

The Comedy Festival also maintained its growth with an interestingly even mix this year between dramatic works (of which TheatreWork's *Full House-No Vacancies* was a memorable example) and anarchic cabaret acts. The *Lawyers, Guns and Money* spoof on the Royal Commission theme, at the Russell Street police auditorium, struck me as being somewhere between the two, and a highlight of the year to boot.

Monodramas continued to

Brian Nankervis regales Valentina Levkowicz with his pipe dreams of stardom.

By
Barbara O'Sullivan

More moving drama from Theatreworks

THE hilarious Theatreworks tradition of moving plays continues with the group's latest production 'Full House:No Vacancies,' directed by Robin Laurie.

Written by Paul Davies, who also penned the hits 'Storming Mont Albert-St Kilda by Tram,' 'Breaking Up in Balwyn' and 'Living Rooms', the show takes place in a series of rooms in the stately mansion 'Linden' in Acland Street St Kilda.

The historic building has been transformed into the rather seedy run down private hotel,'The Linga Longa'.

The audience is divided into groups which, by turns, tour the rooms, viewing a slice of life of the motley collection of residents.

Presided over by manic caretaker Morrey (Phil Sumner), they include Gareth, a deregistered doctor from Wales, (Merfyn Owen), Freddy Finally, a stand-up comic with a confidence crisis (Brian Nankervis), Rosie, a reformed prostitute, (Carolyn Howard) and Sheila, a fading star (Valentina Levkowicz).

Added to this crazy assortment are visitors Liz, a nurse with a yen for travel and an expectant mother (Laura Lattuada) and ruthless property developer Nick (Roger Selleck).

Like many of Davies' pieces, this is funny, boisterous and thoroughly entertaining theatre with a social conscience. It rates as one of the highlights of this month's Comedy Festival.

To book, telephone BASS 11 500 or 650 1977.

The Magazine of the green heart of Australia. Vol.3 No.6 Mar-Apr $3.95

By Lauren Best

At Theatreworks, 14 Acland Street, St. Kilda, in early March, Robert Meldrum will direct 'HORSES', a play adapted by and starring Peter Finlay, which is based on the 'HOUYHNHNN' (pronounced h-wee-nam) section of the brilliant satirical work 'GULLIVER'S TRAVELS' by Swift. Theatreworks will plunge into the start of the 1989 Comedy Festival on the most appropriate day – April 1st – with 'FULL HOUSE – NO VACANCIES' by very popular playwright Paul Davis. Set

in the beautiful old mansion, Linden House, 26 Acland Street, Paul and the Theatrework's crew will again cleverly take audiences through an hilarious evening's 'location theatre' to meet the 'boarding house belt' and the characters who dwell within. If it is anything like Paul's previous sell-out plays, you'll be guaranteed a great night's entertainment, even if you're not a regular theatre buff. For bookings ring 534 8986.

The Emerald Hill, Sandridge and St Kilda Times

Circulating throughout the cities of Port Melbourne, South Melbourne and St Kilda

Vol. 12 No. 12 — 79 Bay Street, Port Melbourne 3207. Phone: (03) 646 5040 — 6 April

It's live-in theatre

WE arrived at the Linga Longa Boarding House in St Kilda only be met by the sign "Full House, No Vacancies".

After some deliberation with the caretaker, Morrie, an objectionable little man, the group was divided into three and ushered into various rooms. We waited patiently in the room of frustrated stand-up comic, Freddie.

FULL HOUSE, NO VACANCIES
Written by Paul Davies.
Theatreworks
Linden Gallery,
26 Acland Street, St Kilda.
Review:
CLAIRE FITZPATRICK

THEATRE

Such an introduction sets the scene for a riotous evening of laughter and innovative theatre. An array of eccentric characters, including a Welsh freedom fighter in a gorilla suit and a dodgy real estate agent, pop in and out of the rooms as the story unfolds, giving a taste of life in a St Kilda boarding house.

Written by Paul Davies, *Full House, No Vacancies* is a clever piece of theatre which induces total audience involvement. Scenes are played to the three groups as they move from room to room.

The story is simple, touching on the topical issues of development in St Kilda which threatens to engulf the Linga Longa. It is laced with limp moralism which reaches its climax in the final scene.

This takes the form of a Happy Hour, where all is revealed in a cabaret.

Overall it makes for great entertainment and an hilarious night out and gets people involved in the true spirit of theatre.

FULL HOUSE
no vacancies

(last night at the "Linga Longa")

BY PAUL DAVIES

Laugh your way from room to room in an actual former St. Kilda Boarding House! From the team that brought you **"Living Rooms"** and **"Storming St. Kilda By Tram"**!

AT "LINDEN"
26 ACLAND STREET ST. KILDA

MONDAYS–SATURDAYS 8.30pm;
MATINEES WEDNESDAY 1.30PM, SATURDAY 5PM
ENQUIRIES: 534 8986   BOOKINGS: 11500 or 650 1977

TheatreWorks is assisted by the Performing Arts Board of the Australia Council. The Federal Government's arts advisory and funding body; the Victorian Ministry for the Arts; the City of St. Kilda.

FULL HOUSE/NO VACANCIES

Gather at the Linga Longa Private Hotel, a run-down, but once historic, boarding house situated at 26 Acland Street, St Kilda. Meet the wealth of 'St Kilda eccentrics' who pop in and out of the rooms ...

Meet MORREY, the blind caretaker who loathes his guests! Wait with faded star SHEILA for 'that' phone call from her agent. Listen to FREDDIE FINALLY's jokes and realise why he didn't get to Edinburgh! Try to understand the lilt of Welsh freedom fighter GARETH, who's lost his passport. Ponder the motives of real estate agent NICK ... did he buy the building? Why? Work out LIZ's guilty secret! Investigate the gorilla suit in ROSIE's cupboard!

The audience moves from room to room as the play unfolds and they piece together the story. The audience is divided into three groups for this purpose, and they gather together for the final scene in the TV Lounge to witness the last Happy Hour at the Linga Longa!

FULL HOUSE: NO VACANCIES is the latest comedy from Paul Davies, who wrote the highly successful Living Rooms, On Shifting Sandshoes, and Storming St Kilda By Tram, the mobile hit of the 1988 Comedy Festival!

Director Robin Laurie
Cast: Carolyn Howard, Laura Lattuada, Valentina Levkowicz, Brian Nankervis, Merfyn Owen, Roger Selleck, Phil Sumner.

Proudly sponsored by SIO STATE INSURANCE OFFICE

FULL HOUSE: NO VACANCIES is an Age Comedy Festival event

VENUE: "LINDEN", 26 ACLAND STREET, ST KILDA
YES!!! It takes place in an actual former St Kilda Boarding House!

Monday – Saturday 8.30pm,
also matinees Wednesday 1.30pm and Saturday 5pm

$19.99 & $15.99 (Wednesday matinees $10.99)

Group concessions available ..... ENQUIRIES 534 8986
From APRIL 3 for a strictly limited season
BOOKINGS: BASS 11500 OR 650 1977

Back of "Linden" 1989   Photo Ruth Maddison

Paul Davies is an award winning screenwriter, script editor and playwright who sharpened his quill on over a hundred episodes of Teledrama from classic Crawford series such as *Homicide* (1974-5), *The Box* (1975-76) *The Sullivans* (1976-78) and *Skyways* (1979), to *Rafferty's Rules* (1985), *Blue Heelers* (1997), *Pacific Drive* (1996), *Stingers* (1998-2003), *Something in the Air* (1999-2001) and *Headland* (2005). He also helped spark the site-specific performance revolution in Melbourne in the 1980s with TheatreWorks' production of his first play *Storming Mont Albert By Tram* (1982). What became known as *The Tram Show* played across a dozen years to packed trams in both Melbourne and Adelaide, travelling a total distance that would have taken the show halfway round the world. Its success lead to an outbreak of 'location theatre' in Melbourne throughout the 1980s including three other plays in real places: *Breaking Up In Balwyn* (1983, on a riverboat), *Living Rooms* (1986, in an historic mansion) and *Full House/No Vacancies* (1989, in a boarding house). These works became the subject of his thesis *Really Moving Drama*.

Both *The Tram Show* and *On Shifting Sandshoes* (1988) were awarded AWGIES, along with *Return of The Prodigal* (2000) an episode of *Something In The Air* (ABC). Paul co-wrote the feature *Neil Lynn* with David Baker in 1984, and the docu-fiction *Exits* (1980) with Pat Laughren and Carolyn Howard. His novel, *33 Postcards From Heaven* was published by Gondwana Press in 2005. Numerous articles, reviews, stories and interviews have been published in *Metro, Cinema Papers, Cantrill's Filmnotes, Australasian Drama Studies, Community Theatre In Australia, The Macquarie Companion to the Australian Media* and *Theatre Research International* (Cambridge University). He co-wrote three documentaries with John Hughes (*All That Is Solid, Traps and One Way Street*) as well as *Holy Rollers* with Rosie Jones. Paul has also given courses in literature and creative writing at various colleges and universities including: Southern Cross, James Cook and Melbourne State.

CAZ HOWARD (1952 – 1990)
Actor, Manager, Co-founder of TheatreWorks

www.ingramcontent.com/pod-product-compliance
Lightning Source LLC
Chambersburg PA
CBHW071923290426
44110CB00013B/1453